Pull Up A Bc

HMS Ganges and Beyond...

By

Chris Neylan

PublishNation
www.publishnation.co.uk

This, mostly, is a recollection of my time as a young recruit in the Royal Navy. Written for my grandson, Leo, born on the 26th June 2016.

In memory of Pamela Neylan (1954 – 2007)

'Pull up a bollard' is a term used (or which was used) just prior to an 'Old Salt' (experienced story-telling sailor) inviting a captive audience to listen to an anecdotal story.

All the events in the book are true. The characters are real, but I have not used real names except where permission to do so has been obtained. The dialogue did test my memory, so, keeping within the vein of the book, I've had to invent some—but by no means all.

Chris Neylan, BEd (Hons)
September 2018

HMS Ganges – A Brief History

The second ship to bear the name HMS Ganges was a three-decker with three masts, boasted eighty-four guns and was built in Bombay Dockyard in 1821.

Controversially, she was built of teak and heated debates within the Admiralty questioned how a ship-of-the-line could possibly be built with anything other than oak. However, teak proved to be more than satisfactory for the building of ships at that time.

HMS Ganges sailed to Portsmouth in 1822 to be fitted out, and in 1823 began undertaking various commissions. Notably, in 1857, she received the distinction of being commissioned as a flagship. Indeed, she was the last sailing ship to receive that distinctive commission.

In 1865 the Ganges sailed to Devonport to be fitted out as a training ship. She spent some time in Falmouth harbour before moving to Harwich harbour in 1899, still as a training ship.

Across the river Stour from Harwich is Shotley, then a small hamlet. It was to here that boys-under-training would row to take advantage of the open land for recreational activities and rifle-shooting practise.

In 1902 the Ganges moved her moorings to the Shotley side of the river, mainly for practical reasons. Before long, because of the lack of up-to-date amenities and poor conditions, especially the lack of sanitation, on board an aging sailing ship, the Admiralty decided to have a shore-based training establishment built on the cliffs overlooking the Shotley peninsula.

In October 1905, the boys from the sailing ship HMS Ganges marched up Bristol Hill to the village of Shotley Gate in order take up residence in their new, brick-built HMS Ganges.

Almost a year later the old Ganges, waved off by a watching crowd on the waterfront at Harwich, and probably from the ratings and officers of the new Ganges, slipped her moorings and sailed for Chatham, becoming part of another training institution.

She was finally paid off at Devonport in 1929 and scrapped. That was the end of a proud career, but some of her timbers remain as part of the main staircase at the National Maritime Museum in Greenwich.

As the number of boys joining Ganges increased, the establishment grew to accommodate them. During the 1950's and 60's there were an estimated 2000 juniors (the rate of 'boy' changed to the rate of 'junior' in 1956) under training at any given time.

The raising of the school leaving age from 15 to 16 in 1972, and a decline in recruitment, brought about the end of HMS Ganges. The White ensign was lowered for the last time in 1976.

There is no disputing that HMS Ganges was a tough, unforgiving, training establishment. Nevertheless, the majority of Juniors who endured the harsh regime, and left to pursue a career at sea, would never forget their time there and, like myself, be proud of once being a Ganges lad.

Recruitment

The sea has, since my very early years, been a source of both escapism and fascination. As a family we would spend holidays in a chalet-type holiday home by the sea in Flamborough, North Yorkshire. We were driven there by a mate of my dad in the back of his old and windowless Morris van. The girls had a monopoly on the cushions; the boys took turns sitting on each other.

Kirkby Avenue School was situated in the village of Bentley, Doncaster—a fifteen-minute walk from my home in Scawthorpe—and I had a mate who lived in a bungalow opposite the school. His dad had been in the Royal Navy and during our final year of school we would spend the dinner hour at his bungalow, sifting through his dad's issues of navy-related periodicals.

Reading through them and being somewhat in awe at the pictures of fighting ships, the men manning them, and my love of the sea, inspired me to respond to one of the many recruitment advertisements they contained.

Doncaster, in 1968, was an industrial town, dominated by the many coal mines and factories dotted around the borough. In the secondary (not-so-modern) schools, male pupils accepted that these were the only viable options open to them for work, and would begin their working life on a shop floor or, like myself, follow their father down a mine. Grammar school pupils fared a little better, with more chance of obtaining an apprenticeship.

The school I attended had factory and pit managers 'touting for business' during Career Days, which started immediately after we entered our fourth and final year—many of us still aged fourteen. So the choice was mine: dull drudgery and lung damage, or excitement on the sea? (I know—sounds like a vibrant coastal town.)

March 1968

My footsteps echoed from the walls and ceiling of the ginnell which separated our house from next door as I trudged home, weary from yet another dreary and reluctant day spent at school. I turned left through the hand-built wooden gate, which was, in fact, more metal than wood: my dad firmly believed that six-inch nails were an essential contribution to any aspect of DIY. Past the large back window then, and with my back to the coalhouse, I let myself into the home I shared with my parents and seven siblings, ranging in age from ten to eighteen years old.

Our home was a four-bedroomed pit house, owned by the National Coal Board. My parents had the large back bedroom. The largest bedroom at the front, with a bunk bed and two single beds, was occupied by my four sisters. Steve and Tim, the youngest of the family, had a bunk bed in the small back bedroom and I shared the small front bedroom with my elder brother, Andy. He had the top bunk—he was the eldest.

'We've had a letter from the Navy,' my mum told me, identifying which of her children had returned from school or work. 'You've to go to that Army recruitment place in town for an interview.'

An interview, crikey - it was only a few weeks ago since I'd been in the recruitment office and handed in my application to join the Royal Navy. There wasn't a Navy recruitment place in Doncaster. Maybe we were too far from the sea, or sharing armed forces recruitment offices was a cost-cutting obsession, even in those days.

My mother seemed as shocked at me getting an interview as she was when she'd learnt that a woman across the road had been seen eating cornflakes in the afternoon.

'Show this letter to your teacher—I don't want any more of those truant letters.'

In the late afternoon, a few days later, I entered the recruitment office and was met by a petty officer (I know the different ranks now; I didn't then) who invited me to sit down opposite him at a rather over-large desk. He explained that I would have to complete various written ability tests, but not to worry because almost every applicant passed.

After about fifteen minutes of brain-wracking and ticking boxes I came to the English test. The petty officer looked over my shoulder and asked me to spell 'beautiful'. I was rather proficient with English as a school subject so spelt beautiful beautifully. He then asked me to nip out and get him a packet of Woodbine cigarettes, waving aside my concerns that I'd not finished all the test sheets with a reassurance that I'd receive a pass. (This must be the reason for the phenomenal pass rate: presumably, those who failed couldn't find a tobacconist.)

When I returned with the cigarettes, and change from a ten-bob note, I was told that I had indeed passed the ability tests for entry as a junior seaman, and handed a sealed letter for my parents, with a place, time, and date to attend a medical concealed within. Then, with a 'good luck' variation of goodbye, I was ushered outside.

Upon reaching home I proffered the sealed envelope to my mother, who was busy in the kitchen preparing tea.

'Father!' she shouted—not the usual 'Tommy.' After all, this was an official-looking envelope requiring an equally official summons. 'Christopher's back from the recruiters, with a letter.'

'Well, open it, then,' came the predictable reply from the front room settee.

After further letter-opening shouted negotiations, it was eventually opened by my dad at the tea/dinner/breakfast/minor injuries treatment table.

'Manchester!' my dad exclaimed. 'One of us has to go with our Chris to Manchester, for his Navy medical.'

'That'll be you, then,' another predictable reply. 'I've enough on looking after these,' her eyes scanning, in age order, the eight children sitting at the table, ending with a steely stare, reserved for my dad.

'Yeah, I knew that before I opened me gob. But it'll be a day out; haven't had one of them for ages—I'll have to put a rest day in.' With that his left arm shot out to rescue my sister, Jane, whose eyes were tightly shut, concentrating so hard as to where Manchester might be she'd almost fallen off her chair.

A month later, at Doncaster station, my dad and I swapped Royal Navy travel warrants for tickets and boarded a train bound for Manchester. My dad had made an effort and was wearing his wedding and funeral shoes and his only suit.

This was, for both of us, a first ever train journey—travelling by bus was a preferred option because we didn't stray too far into the wider world. And it proved to be a memorable and fraught experience.

Even before the train had left Doncaster my dad ignored the no-smoking signs—opening a window, as far as he was concerned, declared them null and void—much to the consternation of other passengers. One, who was particularly disgruntled, went to find a figure of uniformed authority.

A ticket inspector duly arrived and, after a heated debate, we were forced to either find a smoking carriage or get off the train.

Not even bothering to find a smoking carriage—that would be admitting defeat—my dad spent most of the journey with his head through a train-door window. I was leaning on the corridor wall behind him, hoping not to see him collapse into the doorway—minus his head.

5

At the medical centre my dad made it clear to the doctor, before he'd had a chance to remove his stethoscope from his neck, that, despite my pigeon chest, I was fit and healthy, played football and cricket for my school, and always did well on school sports days. Not mentioning that he'd never attended any of my football or cricket matches or, indeed, any sports days.

But my dad wasn't ungenerous. A few days earlier he had won twenty-five quid on the 'Sezue's', a lottery kind of thing, at the local Mine Workers Welfare club.

After my medical, killing time before the return train journey, we browsed the shops in Manchester's centre.

'Owt you want, our Chris?' blunt, as always, asked my dad.

'Well, our English teacher plays classical music during her lessons and…'

'Music, when you're supposed to be learning English?'

'Helps us concentrate, she sez.'

'No wonder you're…'

'Dad, forget it.'

'No, no, if you want some music, I'll buy you some music, if that's what you want. Thought some football boots or sneakers might be better, but…'

My favourite music at the time, well, classical-wise, was *The Planets*, by Gustav Holst. My dad duly bought it for me, but later, at home, I had a hell of a time fighting my elder sisters over use of the record player.

Needless to say I passed the medical (without having to run any errands), and a few weeks later, through the post, received my joining orders, plus a railway warrant. The joining orders dictated that, not even a month after my fifteenth birthday, I would board another train to be turned from a boy into a man.

9 a.m., Tuesday, August 13th 1968

I arrived for the beginning of my Royal Navy career in Sheffield and, after asking for directions, made my way to the Royal Navy recruitment office near Castle Market. All I had with me, as stipulated by way of yet another official letter, was a large cloth bag which contained a toothbrush, a comb, wash bag, change of underwear, my only pair of swimming trunks, and my only pair of football boots.

'You must be Master Neylan,' was assumed by way of a welcome from a chief petty officer as I walked through the door. Without waiting for confirmation he offered me a seat. 'You're the only lad joining from here today,' he told me, 'and the train to King's Cross leaves soon so we'd better get you to the station.'

So we quickly walked back the way I had come not five minutes earlier. Having had my ticket pierced we walked to the correct platform. The CPO told me I should look out for another CPO (he dangled the three-buttoned sleeves of his uniform in my face for identification effect) on arrival at King's Cross who would look after me from there.

I boarded the London-bound train, found a seat (you could in those days), sat down, and wondered what on earth I was doing as the train chugged out of the station in the opposite direction from the place I'd called home for fifteen years.

After alighting the train at King's Cross I spotted a uniformed man on the concourse, at the end of the platform, who was acting 'mother hen' to about ten young lads. After I'd surrendered my one-way ticket and identified three sleeve buttons, I tentatively swelled the group to about eleven just as the CPO looked up from his clipboard.

'And you make fourteen,' he said, pointing to me then ticking, with a flourish, the piece of paper on his clipboard. He was obviously proud of achieving his objective for the day; conversely I was disappointed with my estimating skills.

'Come with us, Mr Neylan, you lot have a coach to catch.' From Master to Mr in three hours—things were looking up!

Again, without conformation of my identity, I joined the other young lads and dutifully followed Mother Hen out of the station and boarded a blue coach with 'RN' printed boldly on each side.

'Settle down now, lads,' said Mother Hen as we band of apprehensive new recruits found seats—which were really wooden benches covered in sticky plastic. 'This coach will take you all the way to Ganges. In that box on the back seat,' he pointed to the back, just in case some or all of us might be geographically inept, 'are some sandwiches and drink. We think of everything, we servants of the Queen, so tuck in when you're ready. Soon be there, my lads, soon be there.'

And with a you-don't-know-what-you're-letting-yourselves-in-for chuckle, he stepped off the coach.

Shotley Gate

The long journey on a rattle-bag of a coach had been more or less uneventful; stopping occasionally for the toilet and a sneaky fag. In fact the offering and sharing of cigarettes initiated some sharing of names, where we were from, and the like, and some early, tentative relationships were formed.

If we'd been apprehensive, nervous, and somewhat frightened of what we might encounter as our coach drove through the Ganges Annexe gates, the bellowing voice that greeted us as we alighted only served to reinforce those emotions. Even the noisy diesel cough of the departing coach failed abysmally to drown the noise being made by the suited and shiny-booted chief petty officer performing the bellowing. And what a performance!

'Line up, single file, single file!' shouted Shiny Boots. 'Single file means one behind the other—are you all thick or stupid or both?' Obviously a rhetorical question because, without waiting for an answer, we were manhandled into an orderly line. (Indeed, throughout my training at Ganges it became the norm for most questions asked by 'those who must be obeyed' to be rhetorical.)

'Follow me, follow me,' continued Shiny Boots. 'You can at least do that, can't you?'

We lived up to his expectations and dutifully followed him, in single file, into a large dormitory-type building that had two long rows of single, metal-framed beds, separated by a walkway. 'This,' continued Shiny Boots, 'is what we in the service call a messdeck. Find a bed, put your bag on it, and follow me for some lovely Pussers grub—in single file!'

Pusser, I later learnt, was a name given to anything supplied by the RN.

Pussers grub turned out to be quite good. We ate in a large dining hall that was to the left of our messdeck's main door.

After eating we filed back to the mess and were told to stand at the side of the bed we had chosen earlier. I must give some credit to Shiny Boots here: he wasn't impervious to how we must all be feeling, and this was demonstrated by his now quiet voice and reasonable manner—almost grandfatherly... almost.

'Now then, lads, it's been a long day for all of you so it's time to turn in and get some sleep.' Turn in? There was a quizzical look on all our faces, but we soon learnt what it meant. 'As you can see, to keep you nice and snug you have a sheet, pillow, and blanket. So, in your own time'—that was a Ganges first and last—'make your bed and, because you've arrived here late, something to do with a train cock-up, and you've yet to have a kit issue, you'll sleep in your underwear.' Before a few hands being tentatively raised reached shoulder height: 'If you ain't wearing any I recommend that your sheet is firmly secured between your soft flesh and the blanket. So make your bed... wait for it... wait for it... you can put your clothes on top of your locker when you've undressed, then turn in. Well, what are you waiting for?'

So we made our bed, undressed, and 'turned in'.

'In the morning you'll be turned out'—turned out made sense—'by your instructor. He'll sort you out with everything else. The more observant of you will have noticed the washroom and heads—toilets to you—as you came in. Those not so observant, head for the dimmed light through this door,' he turned and pointed to the door. 'Get as much kip as you can, you'll need it.' He turned and left the mess, turning off the lights as he departed.

'We didn't get the chance of a wash,' said a voice from a bed. 'I always have a wash before I go to bed. How come we weren't given a chance to wash?' His question went unanswered because none of us had an answer.

I spent most of that first night full of trepidation: what was 'everything else'? What would the next day bring? I felt completely lost, alone, and a little homesick until I heard whispered curses, groans, and some obvious weeping. I found some comfort in realising that I wasn't the only one fretting about the future, and finally drifted into a fretful sleep.

The Annexe

The Annexe was a separate initial-training complex, situated just five minutes double marching time from HMS Ganges' main establishment.

Buildings enclosed a square parade ground—complete with the obligatory mast that all Royal Navy shore establishments contained. Facing each other, on opposite sides of this concreted square of suffering and torment, were three messdecks. Behind the mast were the slops room (clothing store), instructor's mess, and administration buildings. Opposite were the galley, dining hall, and a few classroom-type buildings.

'OH WHAT A BEAUTIFUL MORNING, OH WHAT A BEAUTIFUL DAY, I HAVE THE LOVELIEST FEELING COS BREAKFAST'S A JIFFY AWAY... OUT OF YOUR PITS, SHOW A LEG, SHOW A LEG!'

I was woken by some extremely loud-singing maniac asking me to show him one of my legs whilst scrambling out of a pit, as he walked up and down the mess thrashing the end of beds with a stick. At least the singing had stopped. He must have been some kind of musical aficionado because singing was how he made his morning presence known for the next four weeks.

'Stand by your bed, stand by your bed.' At least his shouty voice wasn't as loud as his singing. 'Morning, my little rays of sunshine. I'm Petty Officer Instructor Green'—we came to call him Teresa—behind his back, of course—'and I'll be your instructor, mother, father, and the best friend you've ever had for the next four weeks. AND YOU WILL CALL ME SIR— AT ALL TIMES. Now, breakfast is waiting, breakfast is waiting, get dressed, quick as you can, quick as you can'—did he live alone with a parrot?—'and use the heads if you have to.'

We struggled into our now very grimy clothes and made good use of the heads. Washing wasn't an option because of the lack of soap and towels. That didn't bother too many of us; even 'the voice from the bed' had no complaints.

'Good, good,' shouted Teresa after we'd all returned to stand by our bed. 'Now, follow me, single file, single file; you're about to be fed, then made official!'

We dutifully followed our instructor to the dining hall. This time, instead of last night's plated meal, we helped ourselves to what was on offer. I'd never had a cooked breakfast before, closest was dipping bread into my dad's bacon fat, so heaped my plate with bacon, sausage, and all other things greasy, then topped it all with baked beans. There were even cereals if you wanted them.

This social gathering inevitably led to conversations, albeit mostly questions and answers, and relationships were beginning to form. Indeed, this is where I 'bonded' with (who was to become my best mate) Alan Harris—'Bomber' as inevitably he became known to his mess-mates, and 'Tweedy', as inevitably he became known to every subsequent instructor.

Teresa gathered his flock after breakfast and lined us up alongside the green, corrugated iron-clad squat building, which was the administration block.

'Now, my lads, you're going to join the Navy proper.'

'I thought we had,' whispered Bomber, but not as quietly as he'd thought.

'No, no, no,' barked Teresa. 'Your mummy and daddy only gave permission for you to get your idle backsides here! Now YOU have to put YOUR monikers on the important bits of paper so I, God help me, can turn you into something fit to serve in Her Majesty's Navy.'

'Will there be a test?' asked another brave soul.

'Will there be a test WHAT?'

'You know, a test like.'

'I know what a ruddy test is! You didn't call me SIR!'

'Sorry errr…'

'Just be quiet and sit down, sit down all of you, sit down and keep your brains warm; there might be a long wait if gash 'ead here is anything to go by.' Gash—Navy speak for rubbish.

So we settled on our haunches and then, as they became cramped and painful, our bottoms.

And now we had a recruitment speech, a speech I'm sure wouldn't go down in recruitment speech annals.

'Now listen to me,' shouted Teresa, strutting up and down our seated line of the bewildered. 'Before the ink is dry on that bit of paper you're going to sign, if you sign it, you'll be mine, all mine. I'm going to turn you into something resembling a fit, clean, smart, and disciplined Royal Navy junior rating! You will all do as I say and do it right—first time—or you'll be sorry!'

Teresa stopped, stooped and faced us. 'And you will call me SIR,' glaring at the brave soul. 'If you want to be treated like mummy and daddy treat you, go back to where you came from!

If you don't want to be here, stand up and get to the back of the line and we'll have you sent home—UNDERSTOOD?'

Nobody moved, nobody dared, nobody would admit to being petrified and wanting to go home: losing face in front of the others, even after such a short time together, was unthinkable. So none of us took up Teresa's generous offer, but some, including myself, wished we had.

After what seemed an eternity the first soon-to-be junior rating (second class) was swallowed by the corrugated iron.

My turn duly came and I found myself sitting at a small table opposite yet another CPO. He confirmed who I was, so this bit must be really important, I thought. He shuffled a pile of papers, set them down neatly, and worked through them methodically, ticking boxes and writing notes as I attempted to correctly answer his questions.

'And now, my lad, before you sign up officially,' said the grave-looking, yet affable-toned CPO, 'you must understand and agree to what I'm going to tell you. So listen very carefully.'

His last sentence reminded me of Herman's Hermits, but I didn't sing out loud.

'You are obliged to serve for three years,' he continued. 'After those three years, when you reach age eighteen, you will be obliged to serve another nine years, making twelve years service in total. Understood?'

'Yes, sir.' I replied, not truly understanding what 'obliged' actually meant. But I was about to have the meaning made abundantly clear.

'Obliged, in this case, means you will,' continued the CPO, a stern tone adopted now, 'serve twelve years, and only the Navy, NOT YOU, will determine whether or not to discharge you as unfit for further service before that time expires. Clear?'

'Yes, sir, clear, sir,' I responded, trying hard to envisage twelve years.

'Sign here, then,' said the CPO, volunteering a pen.

After signing my life (as I knew it) away I was handed my *Guardians of Freedom* booklet, which contained advice and numerous points to remember if I was to become a valued member of the Royal Navy community—then dismissed.

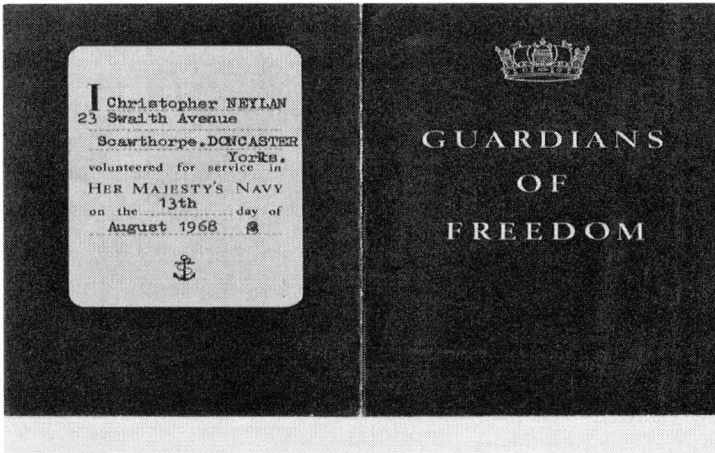

I joined the line of newly promoted junior ratings (second class) waiting outside, and sat next to Bomber. He eased into a conspiratorial-looking pose and whispered, 'Did you get twelve years?'

'Yeah, twelve.'

'Me too.' This was beginning to sound like two newly convicted criminals sharing a cell. 'But it said in one of my letters that I can buy my freedom for twenty quid after I've been here for a few months. He never mentioned that bit.'

'Yeah, it said the same in mine, and he never mentioned it either.'

'You going to?'

'Twenty quid? Fat chance. More than me dad's pay for a week. Anyway, after a few months we might not want to leave.'

'Suppose so.' He pointed to a new line of bewildered young lads.

'Been loads more getting off coaches since I came out.'

'Did Teresa shout at them, too?'

'Nah, somebody else did…'

Speak of the devil…

'My lot, my lot, line up behind me, behind me, NOW. We have six more nozzers'—that's us: the lowest of the low in the RN—'who can't wait to join us in Tiger mess. But before we can welcome them into our family we have to get you all looking, if not acting, like junior ratings. Kitted out is what we call it, kitted out, so follow me, single file, single file, and the slops boys will get you kitted out. Follow me, follow me.'

Inside the slops room and to our right was a long, wide counter with brown-smocked men awaiting behind it. We travelled down the counter and were either asked our sizes or overestimations were taken. 'Don't worry, you'll grow into it,' was an often-repeated phrase. Our heads, to accommodate our hats, were the only part of our bodies to be measured. Six and five-eighths my head measured, and it was never to change, unlike the rest of me.

Our kit consisted of everything we needed for our initial four weeks' training: wash bag with a toothbrush, a razor (with two spare blades) and a shaving brush contained within. Three pairs of underwear, three white vests, pyjamas, boots (two pairs), boot brushes (of varying stiffness), boot polish, socks, stockings, working shirts and trousers (No. 8s—three pairs), a pair of overalls, one belt, two hats, towels, four sheets, four pillow cases, sports shirts and shorts (one blue, one white), white plimsolls, white Blanco, deck shoes (slippers, sort of), handkerchiefs, gloves, a large khaki tubular-shaped canvas kitbag with draw strings, enamelled mug, and housewife (a folding cloth bag with two pockets containing every conceivable item used for sewing and darning).

The last item of issue was a wooden block with a type of my name arranged at one end.

'Name?'

'Neylan, sir.'

'Initial?'

'Err, N, sir.'

'You sure? Says C on 'ere.'

'Well, err, Neylan starts with a capital N, sir.'

'Give me strength… what's your first name, your Christian name, what your mother calls you?'

'Oh, that's Christopher, sir.'

'Gawd, I hope you're not in the Signals branch. Move on, move on.'

Pity we both didn't check my entire name.

'All done?' queried Teresa as silence and stillness invaded the slops room.

'They've all they need for now,' replied one of the brown-smocked men. 'Them still 'ere will get rest int big place.'

'Now then, Tiger mess,' Teresa barked as he assumed his usual, authoritarian position, fronting the line of the even more bewildered, 'open that big round bag and carefully, carefully stow your kit inside. NOW, CHOP, CHOP!'

We stowed our kitbags as carefully, yet as quickly as we could—no one wanted to be last, tempting Teresa's wrath.

Teresa scanned the line of junior ratings, waiting for us to finish stowing. Satisfied that stowing was complete, he demonstrated, with the nearest bag, how to tighten the drawstrings and secure them with a flick-of-the-wrist knot.

'See how easy that was? Secure your kitbags!' Of course, we all used two hands to attempt a knot similar to the demonstrated one.

'What a shambolic lot you are! Never mind, never mind, knots is what you'll be learning in the proper Ganges IF any of you make it there! Pick up your bags and single file outside, outside, NOW!'

Once outside, in single file, Teresa shared with us his first of many pearls of naval wisdom.

'Now then, before we walk, yes, walk, because you can't even begin to think you know how to march, you're going to heave those kitbags onto your left shoulder and secure them with your left arm. Do any of you nozzers know why it's the left shoulder?' Silence. 'Because, because, your right arm is used to salute officers, the flag of this esteemed realm, and the quarterdeck. You can't salute with your right arm if it's full of kitbag, can you? Now, lift and secure, lift and secure, and if anything falls out you'll wish you were back home with Mummy and Daddy! Lift and secure!'

We grabbed and lifted, furtively confirming left from right by looking at others. The kitbag wasn't too heavy, even for my somewhat diminutive stature. If we'd been issued with all the kit required to serve as a fully-fledged naval rating, it would have been a different, miserable story.

Back in Tiger mess we'd emptied our kitbag, spreading the contents on our bed, noticing the large cardboard box at the foot of it.

Teresa nodded to himself. 'Now's the time to LOOK like nozzers! From your kit get a No. 8 shirt, No. 8 trousers, underpants, a pair of socks, boots, and a towel.' To avoid any confusion he held up the items as he spoke. 'Good, good. Now strip, take everything, everything, off, and stuff it into your cardboard box.'

A timid voice expressed his concern: 'Everything?'

Teresa, his face flushed with annoyance, shouted, 'Everything MEANS everything. And you didn't call me SIR!'

What happened next was a cruel example of the humiliation most of us would endure during our time at Ganges.

Teresa strode over to the unfortunate offender. 'Your name?'

'Reed... sir, Sam Reed... sir.'

Teresa kicked Sam's box into the middle of the mess. 'Now, lad, take ALL your civvies off and PUT them in that ruddy BOX—NOW! You nozzers who didn't understand EVERYTHING, watch and learn, watch and learn!'

Poor Sam paled, his complexion becoming more pallid as he stripped, dropping each item into his cardboard box. Socks in the box and down to his underpants, he hesitated.

'Don't be shy, lad, don't be shy. GET THOSE CRACKERS OFF AND IN THAT RUDDY BOX!'

Sam, now a rosy-red colour, slipped off his 'crackers' and dropped them in his box.

'Now, lad, get yourself over here, in front of me,' shouted Teresa. 'Stand to attention! Feet together, arms by your side, and stick that pathetic chest out! All of you take a good look at what EVERYTHING means. Civvies in the box, in the box, NOW!'

So we all stripped, dropping our civvies into a box, sharing Sam's embarrassment but not his humiliation.

'And now,' said Teresa, his shouting a few decibels lower, 'and now you're going to get showered and dressed, dressed into your No. 8s. So grab your towels, wrap them round your waist, and line up in single file.'

When we had successfully ordered ourselves into single file Teresa concluded his instructions. 'In the drying room is a box of soap. As you go through the drying room take a bar of soap then get a shower. There are only six showers so don't hang about! I want to see all you nozzers clean, dressed, and standing to attention at the side of your bed in... what shall we say... twenty minutes. At the double, at the double—GET ON WITH IT!'

Teresa strode up and down the mess, reluctantly satisfied with our showering and dressing but whinging about his workload. 'Normally, normally, there's a junior instructor deployed to each mess who sleeps in here and helps me with your training. BUT because you lot joined us at the start of Ganges summer leave, I have to do it ALL BY MYSELF!' His rant was cut short by a man in a green smock coughing at the mess door.

'All set up and ready, PO.'

'Thanks, Cyril, won't be long,' acknowledged Teresa. 'Single file, single file, follow me, follow me.'

Teresa led us towards a small room near the dining hall. One after the other we were ushered inside and had our hair cut. Well, not so much cut, but sheared like sheep—scissors didn't play any part in the process.

Back in the mess Teresa gathered us round and demonstrated the art of tying the HMS Ganges cap tally onto our caps. It would have taken ages, and no doubt elicited another 'all by myself' rant from Teresa, if it wasn't that some mess mates had been in the Sea Cadets. They helped with the tying of bows, cutting the end of the tally into an introverted V shape and sewing in the itchy chinstraps, enabling a hurricane-proof fit.

The help with the tallies and chinstraps seemed to have improved Teresa's mood. 'Dinner time! Go to the heads if you have to, wash your hands, and line up, single file, single file outside! You'll get your kit marked and properly folded after dinner. Your civvies will be collected and sent back to your mummy, so make sure you've tied the address label on your box securely! Chop chop!'

Like breakfast, dinner was also a choice from the hot counter. It was plentiful and very tasty. Truly, like the Army, Ganges believed that its ratings-under-training marched on their stomachs—we didn't walk, saunter, stroll, amble, or meander—we marched everywhere and, more often than not, at the double!

Teresa collected us from the dining hall and we quickly assembled back in Tiger mess. He held up one of the wooden name types and explained its use. Any item of kit of a dark colour was to be stamped with our name in white; lighter colours in black. We would tackle the dark items first because it made sense - switching from white to black was easier.

It was a long and laborious procedure: Teresa displaying every item and where exactly to stamp. It had to be exact to show the name on any to-be-folded items when they were folded—correctly.

We sorted our kit then dipped our types into the white paint provided and commenced stamping.

It wasn't until I'd stamped the inside of my belt that I noticed, alarmingly, that something was wrong, dreadfully wrong: my name's Neylan, NOT Naylan. I turned to a busy-stamping Bomber.

'Hey, Bomber, look at this, my name's wrong.'

'Wrong?'

'Yeah, it's got an A and it should be an E, there, look.'

Bomber looked, breathed in deeply, exhaled dramatically, then pointed out the bleedin' obvious: 'You're in it deep, Lofty'. (I was officially five feet, one and three-quarter inches tall, hence the contradictory nickname.) 'Best let Teresa know and...'

'And what?'

'Don't cry...'

Clutching my belt and full of foreboding, I approached Teresa, At least I remembered how to address him: 'Sir.'

'Have you finished already, lad? Never had you down as a quick worker.'

'No, not finished, sir, something's wrong.'

'Wrong! What can possibly be wrong? It's not ruddy hard; stamping your kit is NOT RUDDY HARD!'

'It's my name, it's spelt wrong, sir.' By now Teresa and I were the centre of attention.

'Show me, show me!'

So I showed him.

'Unbelievable! Ruddy un-believ-able! Did you not check after your first stamp, like I ruddy told you to?'

If he'd told us to do that I couldn't remember but, thinking about it, and much too late, it made sense to do just that.

'I only noticed after I'd stamped my belt, sir, sorry, sir.'

'SORRY, BLEEDIN SORRY!' Face flushed and very angry, Teresa grabbed my shirt front and dragged me to my pile of stamped kit. He looked, he swore, again and again. 'It's a ruddy good job you stopped and didn't get on to black!' Still holding my shirt he dragged me to the top of the mess where the sparkly-clean mess dustbin lived, and lifted off its lid. 'GET IN THERE; STAND TO ATTENTION, STAND TO ATTENTION!'

I stood in the bin and meekly stood to attention. Teresa didn't have to assemble the rest of the mess: they'd already gravitated to the best viewing points.

Teresa turned to our audience. 'This miserable excuse for a naval rating has something he'd like to share with you.' He swivelled on his heels and, prodding me in the chest with a large bony finger, shouted in my face, 'YOU, ARE, A, NOZZER, WHO, DOESN'T, LISTEN! WHAT—ARE—YOU?'

I was like a rabbit caught in headlights. I attempted a reply but all I could manage was a stumbling stutter.

'WHAT ARE YOU?' He reversed his swivel. 'TELL HIM WHAT HE IS, TELL HIM!'

There was a mumbled response. I hoped it was a show of empathy, not that they'd forgotten what Teresa had said.

'TELL HIM HE'S A NOZZER WHO DOESN'T LISTEN! TELL HIM!'

So, with their loudest voice, they told me.

With another reverse swivel, Teresa started again with his prodding. 'WHAT—ARE—YOU?'

'I am a nozzer who doesn't listen, sir.'

'LOUDER!'

'I AM A NOZZER WHO DOESN'T LISTEN, SIR!'

'KEEP SHOUTING IT TILL I TELL YOU TO STOP. KEEP SHOUTING! KEEP SHOUTING!'

I stood in the dustbin and yelled until Teresa saved my vocal chords from permanent damage. 'GET OUT, GET OUT!' He peered inside the dustbin. 'Well, well, well. YOU'VE DIRTIED MY DUSTBIN!'

And so I was ordered to get my toothbrush and soap, and a bucket from the washroom, filled with hot water, and clean the inside of the dustbin. I scrubbed and rinsed, scrubbed and rinsed, then polished using a foul-smelling liquid inappropriately called Bluebell Polish, until Teresa was satisfied that the inside of his beloved dustbin had been returned to all its sparkly glory.

The rest of Tiger mess had been rested from their stamping and were lined up, in single file, ready to go for tea. Teresa took my name type and I put the cleaning things back in their proper place. Luckily for me I still had the toothbrush I'd bought from home: the issued one I'd used looked like it had cleaned the teeth of every horse ridden by John Wayne.

Housewife with incorrect spelling
25

Tea was a buffet-type meal with ready-buttered bread—I had my first sandwich with both slices of bread buttered—and a selection of fillings. I was amazed at the different concoctions of sandwiches made. Indeed, not only had I to get used to regional variations of meal choices, but also accents, turn of phrases, and slang words. However, before long we all spoke the same language: Navy speak!

Back in Tiger mess Teresa drew our attention to a pile of little wooden boxes. These, he told us, were our 'ditty boxes'. We collected a box each and were told to place it on our locker. This box was for the safekeeping of our personal items, such as writing gear, letters, and photographs. But by far the most important items to be kept within were two books: *The Admiralty Manual of Seamanship* and *The Naval Ratings Handbook* (the latter had the shortened name of 'Ships Book').

Teresa commenced to take us into the bewildering world of kit folding. He started by demonstrating the folding of kit that could, and should, and would, be folded 'Ships Book Size'. It would have been easier (but not much) if folding was 'Seamanship Manual Size': this book was about a third larger.

To add further complications the folded kit had to have the owner's name displayed in such a way that, neatly piled in the locker, they would be exactly in line. Needless to say Teresa was duty-bound to point out that the 'Nozzer With No Name' would, without a doubt, fail his first locker inspection.

And so we folded, unfolded, swore, swore again, and sweated over folded and unfolded kit. Teresa left us to it, giving us an hour to practise; leaving us in no doubt that his patience would be sorely tested if Tiger mess lockers didn't pass muster on his return.

Upon his return Teresa, thankfully, took only a cursory glance at our attempts at kit folding and storing: he was more interested in making sure the home address on our civvies-box label was correct, and correctly tied to the box. And he just couldn't let my past error go: 'I hope you, young Neylan, have remembered where you live, and your mummy's name!'

'Tomorrow, tomorrow will be your first lesson in Parade drill! Oh I'm so looking forward to tomorrow! Now, my grubby, would-be junior seaman, grab your mugs, it's time for Kye'—Navy-made cocoa—'before you turn in. Ah, that reminds me: at Call the hands, when you turn out, you'll be shown how to make your bed—the GANGES WAY!'

Kye was dished out from a steaming urn in the dining room. It was thick, hot tasty, and somehow comforting. (Indeed, kye became a welcome part of many a middle and morning watch during my later years at sea.)

Because it was a warm and balmy evening we were allowed to drink our kye outside. It also gave us the chance to swap our early Annexe experiences with lads from different messes, have a smoke, and compare POI's. Apparently they were all of a breed similar to Teresa.

27

Having washed our mugs, washed ourselves, and changed into cardboard pyjamas, we turned in. Two days, two days seemed like two weeks. Bomber obviously had similar thoughts.

'It's only been two days, Lofty. Seems more like two bleedin weeks!'

'Yeah, I was thinking that, but tomorrow's supposed to be better, so Teresa said.'

'Better for him more like. Where you from, Lofty? You sound like one of them geezers off Coronation Street.'

'Doncaster.'

'Where's that, then? Must be up north somewhere.'

'In Yorkshire. Where you from?'

'Norwich.'

'Well, wherever that is you sound like one of them farmers off radio, Archers, me mother listens to it.'

'Yeah, very funny. See you in the morning, Lofty. Roll on breakfast.'

'And Bomber...'

'What?'

'Leave some sausages for the rest of us.'

'Cheeky sod.'

'Keep the bleedin noise down!' The duty POI doing his rounds was as charming as Teresa.

Welcome to the Parade Ground

'THE SUN 'AS GOT 'IS 'AT ON, HE'S SHOUTING HIP HOORAY... IT'S SIX O'CLOCK AND YOU LOT ARE STILL IN YOUR PITS! UP, UP, SHOW A LEG, SHOW A LEG. WASHED AND CHANGED, WASHED AND CHANGED INTO YOUR NUMBER 8's—NOW!'

'Six o'clock, it's only six o'clock,' whispered Ryan Dooly (Paddy) in his broad Irish brogue. He occupied the bed to my left. 'What ruddy time is six o'clock?'

So this was the time we'd have to get used to. None of us knew the time because ALL we possessed, except for swimming trunks and football boots, had gone into that cardboard box. Presumably, using a watch suggested using initiative, and nozzers using initiative wasn't allowed.

As promised, and not one to let us down, Teresa demonstrated the Ganges art—yes, it really was an art—of bed-making. The bed was stripped then the mattress cover pulled taught until no creases showed. The two sheets were folded in a way that showed our name (I was at a disadvantage straightaway) and to exact dimensions. The same with the blanket, which was then placed at the head of the bed, centred on the mattress. The sheets went on top of the blanket and the pillow on top of the sheets. And your bed had to be made correctly, every morning, before you could even think of using the heads or having a wash. When dressed in the dress-of-the-day, pyjamas were folded and stowed in their allocated space in the locker.

Teresa inspected each bed and each rating standing (at attention) at the foot of it. He wasn't best pleased with some

29

nozzers shaving attempts, so they were sent to try again. I hadn't even attempted to shave: a light breeze was enough for me.

After breakfast all messes were intercepted by their respective POI's upon leaving the dining hall and mustered, mess by mess, on different areas of the large parade ground.

Teresa detailed two of our burliest mess members (Bomber being one of them) to collect a large cardboard box, at the double, from a pile stacked against the slops wall. After the box had been dutifully placed at Teresa's feet, he opened it and produced the latest addition to our kit: gaiters. Khaki in colour and about as flexible as Teresa's instructions, gaiters were to be strapped around our ankles, covering the tops of our boots with trousers ballooning from the top. Two straps and buckles eventually, after weeks of being worn, ensured a firm, comfortable fit.

Teresa's next objective was to have us form up in three rows, known as ranks. Because there were twenty of us, the front and rear ranks numbered seven, the middle six. (This was the standard arrangement of mustered ranks in the Navy if the number of men wasn't divisible by three.) With the ranks sorted we now had to arrange ourselves in height order: the tallest on the flanks, the shortest in the middle. I was positioned in the middle of the front rank because, as Teresa pointed out, I couldn't possibly be seen if I stood anywhere else!

Teresa then attempted to teach us the basics of Parade drill: 'Tiger mess, messss HO! Heels together, arms straight down your sides, shoulders back, chins up, chests out!'

He strutted up and down the ranks, whacking legs and shoulders with his stick and theatrically expressing his displeasure with our efforts. Luckily for us the three former Sea Cadets came to our rescue—again. He placed them in front of our ranks: one facing, one sideways, and the other showing his back. Teresa, pointing with his stick, made us very aware of the positioning of hands, feet, chin, head, and shoulders. 'This,' he shouted, 'is the correct and ONLY WAY to stand at ATTENTION! TRY AGAIN!'

After five minutes of body part shuffling, aided by Teresa's bony fingers and whacks from his stick, we resembled, and only just, by Teresa's reckoning, three ranks of attensionised junior seaman (second class).

We then tackled the more demanding aspects of Parade drill: standing at ease, standing easy, and dressing. Dressing is the way that ensures spacing amongst the ranks. At attention, the head swivelled to the right, the right arm was raised to a horizontal position and we shuffled our feet so our clenched fist touched the shoulder of the junior seaman to our right. Easy! Dressing by the left is, obviously, the opposite.

Then moving to the left or right in threes. Moving to the right consisted of swivelling on the right heel then smartly (quickly) bringing the left heel to smack against the right.

At Teresa's shouted command some turned right, others turned left, and some didn't move at all. After much shouting, swearing and manhandling we were now standing at attention and facing the right way. Once again, in order to ease his heavy workload, Teresa took advantage of the sea cadets. They demonstrated the complicated art of marching: arm swinging, keeping in step, wheeling left, wheeling right, and halting.

'Remember, remember,' shouted Teresa, 'always, ALWAYS, step off with your left boot, ALWAYS! Your left boot is the one that's NOT your right boot! Lift your left boots!' We stood, swaying in the sunshine, until Teresa was satisfied with our boot choice.

'Don't cock this up—DO NOT COCK THIS UP!' We stood at a tremble, most of us staring down at our left boot—big mistake! 'GET THOSE HEADS UP!' shouted Teresa whacking his stick across indiscriminate shoulders. 'BY THE LEFT, QUICK MARCH!' Some stepped off with their left boot, others their right, and some, undecided, didn't move at all.

The Sea Cadets sniggered.

Teresa, his face twisted in anger, and with much cursing and shouting, had the class 'as we were': standing at attention and facing him. He stood us at ease. Oh, good, I thought, we're going to have a breather. No such luck.

'Cadets, out front, at the double!' With the smug-looking cadets at his side Teresa began his first and only lesson in left and right discrimination.

'Class, class, remove your left boot and place it behind you—NOW!' So we did. Teresa, making sure the correct boot had been removed, had us stood to attention, dressed and moved to the right in quick order.

We marched, stumbled, marched around the parade ground until Teresa, satisfied with our ever increasing marching prowess, exchanged his cursing and swearing for intermittent 'EFT, IGHT, EFT, IGHT, EFT, IGHT, LERFT, EFT, EFT, EFT, IGHT, LERFT,' keeping in-step guidance. I noticed, as we were attempting to reach Teresa's expectations, all the other Annexe messes suffering in much the same way as we were.

Eventually we came to a halt alongside our abandoned boots. We picked them up with our left hand then stood to attention with the boot arm held up at a 90 degree angle. After a few agonising minutes Teresa, aware of our extreme discomfort, kindly took our mind off that pain by adding another: we bent our knees and sank to our haunches, straightened our knees, then back on our haunches. We bobbed up and down like demented cobblers.

We were finally allowed to return our boot to its proper, uniformed place, telling left from right fully etched into our memories—I can still tell left from right even now. We finished the drill session with Ganges' favourite pastime—double marching.

Because we practised Parade drill over and over again during our time at Ganges, it became a kind of automated second-nature. Even drilling with rifles became just routine. But I never did find out why the command HO!, or sometimes HU! was used to bring us to attention. Didn't sound anything like ATTENTION!

But I fully understood why—we were sailors after all—left and right hadn't been exchanged for port and starboard. What confusion that would have led to!

Having 'drilled' through stand-easy (as well as a parade command, stand-easy was also Navy speak for break), dinner was a very welcome event. Naval ratings didn't do 'lunch'. Lunch was for officers and people who lived in big houses.

After dinner Teresa gave us the rest of the day to finish kit stamping. He gave me my correctly named type and watched, eagle eyed, as I stamped my first item. Satisfied that I recognised the correct spelling of my own name, he left us to it.

The most important items of kit that required stamping were the ones on the white tape, over the left breast pocket on our No. 8 shirts. No. 8s (working dress) were the most frequently worn of all our numbered uniforms, so having your name prominently displayed was advantageous, or disadvantageous, depending on the situation you found yourself in.

One shirt had to have the name sown in with red thread. This shirt had to be worn for specific occasions, such as divisions and pay parade. Teresa had told us that, up until just a few months ago, all kit had to be sewn in. According to him, we'd been let off—big time!

We all 'turned in' at the end of a strenuous and exhausting day, falling into an immediate, deep sleep.

Friday replicated Thursday: Parade drill, kit stamping, folding, and how and where to stow properly folded kit in our locker.

As we turned in that evening the chat revolved around what we'd do at the week-end. All kinds of bizarre suggestions were put forward: from going to the cinema in Ipswich, to walking to the nearest pub for a pint (really). Reality proved to be very different, very different indeed.

We were woken by Teresa's usual ruination of a once popular song. Not satisfied with our 'turning out' speed (we were, after all, anticipating a weekend lie in), he had us double around the parade ground, dressed in pyjamas and boots. Another mess, obviously guilty of a more serious offence, were doubling with bedding on their head.

After breakfast we fell in (three ranks) on the colonnade outside our mess. Teresa introduced us to the weekly ritual of Saturday rounds. Everywhere and everything had to be cleaned: walls, windows, floors, heads, washroom, drying room, our section of the colonnade, and all visible surfaces. We were split into groups and given an area or thing to clean. Much of the cleaning apparatus was unfamiliar to most of the mess, but Teresa eased our concerns by reassuring us that on-the-job instruction would be supplied—in abundance.

Hours later, after scrubbing, mopping, and polishing, all messes were fallen in, at attention, on the parade ground waiting for the divisional officer to commence his Saturday morning inspection.

After all messes had been inspected by the DO he marched himself over to a small dais in front of the mast, stood on it, then shared his thoughts.

'I can see a good effort has been made,' the DO said, in a moderately loud voice. He continued but with his adopted Ganges shouty voice. 'But your efforts were not good enough! Being clean and living in a clean and tidy ship are essential

35

both to the health and well-being of every Royal Navy rank and rating, and the fighting effectiveness of the ships in which they serve! I'll be looking for a vast improvement next Saturday. DO NOT DISSAPOINT ME!'

When we returned to the mess we found it in a reasonable state, compared to what we would find post Saturday rounds in *Ganges Proper*. A few beds had their bedding strewn across the deck, a couple of sheets were hanging from the rafters, the dustbin was upside-down in the washroom, and a few towels were stuffed in toilet bowls. Teresa then delivered his lengthy discipline speech, a speech I would remember and use as a guide throughout my time in the Navy and in later life.

We stood at attention at the foot of our bed as Teresa paraded up and down our now disorderly mess:

'Why is your mess looking as it is now after all your hard work? Well, I'll tell you. It's all about discipline! Discipline rules in the Navy! It means you will obey all orders without question, respect rank and be in obedience to every rule and regulation! And just as important, maybe more important, is self-discipline!' He lifted a blanket from the deck and threw it to join the sheets in the rafters. 'Those belong to nozzers who couldn't be bothered to have a final check. The towels down the heads belong to nozzers who couldn't be bothered to change them for clean ones. Am I getting through? I couldn't be bothered, I'll do it later, or I'll sneak away for a crafty smoke and hope somebody else does it, are but a few examples of lack of SELF-DISCIPLINE! AND IT KILLS!'

He came to rest, sitting on an ironing table. 'Down in that holiday camp they dare call *HMS* Raleigh, where nozzers older than you do their training, a nozzer couldn't be bothered to properly clear his rifle after shooting practise because he was in a hurry to be first at the kye urn. He left a round in the breach. The armourer decided he would check the returned weapons later, after his kye and fag. That round, THAT ROUND KILLED SOME POOR SOD!'

True or just for effect, that story ensured that 'clearing' any weapon I used throughout my service was something I did with due diligence.

He slid off the table and resumed parading. 'When you're in *Ganges proper,* sneaking magazines and newspapers back from shore leave, THINK, when you're in your pit reading the naughty bits in the News of the World, wouldn't it be better if I read my Ships Book, Seamanship manual or text books I've been given from school?' School? Teresa noticed the wealth of puzzled frowns. 'Yes, school. Did you think you were clever enough to be a rating in the Royal Navy? Take my advice and learn, learn everything there is to learn and, above all, be PROUD that you've had enough self-discipline to have been able to do it! Now get this mess looking something like a Ganges mess!'

We set about rectifying Tiger mess, with Teresa offering shouted guidance. Dinner was a muted affair: every Annexe nozzer still reeling from the aftermath of Saturday rounds.

After dinner, and back in the mess, gathered around Teresa and an ironing table, we were given our first of many ironing lessons. Teresa showed us how to iron No. 8s the Ganges way, fold them, and where and how to stow them in our locker. He then produced a photograph of a correctly stowed Ganges locker, taken recently in a mess in *Ganges proper*. 'This is the correct and ONLY way to stow your kit! I'm doing you a BIG favour giving you this, so be grateful; other nozzers only have the picture in their Ships Book to look at!'

Now, looking back, I wasn't sure if Teresa was being uncharacteristically kind, or seeking to be deemed a superior Annex POI. Whatever, his photograph certainly helped.

'Now,' Teresa continued, 'if you don't do anything else this afternoon, give your boots a good polish and make dammed sure the No. 8 shirt with the sewn in name is ironed to perfection: you'll be wearing it at divisions in the morning!' He pinned the life-saving photo on the notice board and left us to our boot polishing, ironing, and locker stowing.

We'd all quickly realised that we were all in this together, so helped each other in any way we could, as Kinky was about to demonstrate.

Boot polishing was another art in itself. Pete King (Kinky), one of the former sea cadets, was cleaning his boots whilst waiting for a place at one of the two ironing tables. Bomber and I, also waiting, looked on in amazement as Kinky wrapped a cleaning rag around one of his index fingers, spat on it, then loaded it with boot polish and began rubbing it, in circular movements, over the toe cap of a boot, occasionally adding more spit directly onto the toe cap.

Aware of his audience, Kinky shared his polishing technique. 'You build up a layer of polish, see,' said Kinky, between spits, 'but it takes a lot of time and polish like, so you have to do it over and over again till it's like looking in a mirror like.'

He was right about the time and polish, but the end results were amazing. Upon joining their first ship, Ganges boys were easily identified by their gleaming, polished boots and shoes.

'What's these divisions, then, Kinky?' asked Bomber.

'Dunno, really,' replied Kinky, mid spit. 'Guessing it's like parades we used to have in the cadets like, when all local areas were inspected by a big chief from somewhere like.' Kinky was obviously from the North West like. 'Guessing all the Annex will parade like.'

'He's right,' butted in Eric White (Chalky). 'Me cousin was ere a few years back. Think he told me it were sumfin like that.'

'They'll be queuing up to shout at us, then.' I said.

'Yeah, guess so,' said Chalky. 'Me cousin went on his first leave and never came back. Never got used to all this shouting malarkey. There's room at ironing tables now.'

'Come on, Lofty,' said Bomber, 'best leave boots for last: don't want a shirt covered in boot polish.' If Bomber had so much common sense, why was he here?

Tea was a much livelier affair with lads from other messes confirming Kinky's understanding of divisions. Teresa didn't bother us again, so it was left to the duty POI to dutifully shout at us until we turned in.

'Hey, Lofty.'
'What?'
'Have you remembered?'
'Remembered what?'
'What's yer left and what's yer right.'
'Sod off, Bomber.'

Divisions

After breakfast, fed, suitably suited and booted, with every mess mustered and fallen-in on their designated places on the parade ground, Divisions commenced.

From the very start a Chief Gunnery Instructor (CGI's—masters in the art of marching and parade drill), his voice box filled with gravel, set about causing immense confusion amongst the ranks: 'Parade! Parade! HO!'

Parade? Is that us? We'd only been addressed as mess, Tiger or otherwise, and mess, unbeknown to us, had been replaced by Parade. Only the former sea cadets sprang to attention, and by the time the rest of us individually cottoned on, the expected gun-shot-thwack of a hundred and twenty boot heels smacking together became sporadic gunfire.

'AS YOU WERE!' shouted the CGI. 'YOU'VE BEEN HERE LONG ENOUGH TO KNOW THE ATTENTION COMMAND! POI's, SORT EM OUT, SORT—EM—OUT!'

Needless to say Teresa was not best pleased. 'STAND ATTA-EASE! BLOOD AND FIRE, BLOOD AND FIRE! WHAT THE BLEEDIN HELL WAS THAT? TODAY, TODAY OF ALL DAYS YOU HAVE TO COCK IT UP! PARADE MEANS YOU, ALL OF YOU. YOU'RE ALL ON BLEEDIN PARADE! ON A BLEEDIN PARADE GROUND! HOW BLEEDIN EASIER CAN IT BE!' His face had turned beetroot red. 'YOU'LL WISH YOU'D STOPPED AT HOME WITH MUMMY BEFORE THIS DAY IS OVER, BELIEVE ME, BELIEVE ME!' Oh, we believed him.

The CGI, once he'd heard enough encouraging shouting, brought us to a reasonably effective attention, facing the mast and the Divisional officer. The DO didn't look at all angry, just wearing a 'just-what-I expected-look. He strolled (yes, strolled, as was his right) up and down the parade ground inspecting each mess. By the time he reached Tiger mess, obviously disillusioned, he gave us just a cursory onceover, said something to Teresa then took his position before the mast.

A vicar, or someone religious, judging by his clothing, climbed onto a small dais. He extolled the virtue of many things (some I'd never heard of), commended us on our choice of career, blessed us, climbed down and disappeared behind the admin block. We were resumed to our attention position, turned hither and thither until we'd adopted our march past formation, then each mess marched past the DO who'd taken the place of the vicar on the dais.

'EYESA LEFT!' barked Teresa as Tiger mess drew level with the DO. Teresa saluted as heads swivelled to the left, then swivelled back when Teresa dropped his salute.

Now that was good, I thought. That went really well thanks to many hours of parade drill practise. Surely that would earn us some atonement for the sinful HO! Wishful thinking.

'Send em round again!' shouted the DO. 'This time I want to see straight lines, straight backs, proper marching, AND YOU ALL DOING THE SAME BLEEDIN THING AT THE SAME BLEEDIN TIME!'

So we went round, again and again. The DO disappeared to wherever DO's disappeared to after divisions and left us to our very unhappy POI's. They took turns in voicing their displeasure, then took turns sending us round again, and again, but this time at the double; the blazing August sun adding to our suffering. Each POI sent us round twice then went off to drown kittens, or whatever they did in their spare time.

The final POI on nozzer-punishment duty, noticing that some were about to die, brought us to a halt and dismissed us to the dining hall.

We were late for dinner, very late, and queued for the water urn, dried meat, congealed gravy, and stewed vegetables. But even the pungent smell of over-boiled cabbage failed to mask the sour smell of over a hundred sweaty bodies. The duty POI, wrinkling his nose, told us to hurry up, return to our mess, shower, change, and look forward to an exciting afternoon. More excitement, how could we cope with more excitement?

The *excitement* turned out to be a routine Sunday afternoon visit to the cinema. The Annexe *cinema* was really a large loft space located somewhere behind Tiger mess, accessed by metal steps. Once inside we sat on very uncomfortable wooden benches and watched Battle of the River Plate, struggling to hear the dialogue above the noise of an ancient projector.

We eventually found out that this was the last film shown to the last Annexe intake, and the only one available because Ganges was on summer leave. So for every following Sunday afternoon's entertainment in the Annexe, we sat and fidgeted through the bravery and tenacity of HMS Exeter, HMS Ajax and HMNZ Achilles, as they forced the German battleship Graf Spee into taking refuge in Montevideo harbour. And poor old Captain Langsdorff blowing his brains out after he'd blown his ship to pieces. Not yet steeped in naval history, we didn't question why he hadn't gone down with his ship.

Life in the Annexe continued with repetitive parade drill, kit mustering, mess inspections, divisions, and various forms of punishment. We made weekly visits to the Annexe laundry room and were shown how to scrub our kit clean in large, Belfast-type sinks using pussers hard: a block of brown soap not given to lathering.

The monotony was finally broken during our third week. We had a medical, were measured for our No. 2 and No. 1 blue serge uniforms, had our pay book issued, complete with photograph, so we could be paid our pittance, and sat the Navy's equivalent of a MENSA test. The test determined which branch of the Seaman Division we would be allocated to.

Divisions were a part of the whole that made up the Royal Navy. There were, amongst others, Stokers (marine engineers) Electricians, Cooks (who liked to be called Chefs), and Signals (bunting tosses).

Seaman were mostly responsible for the upper deck, which included tying the ship to land when we entered harbour, untying it when we left, dropping anchor, weighing it (hauling it back in), steering the ship, look-outs when at sea, lowering, manning and unlowering boats, and keeping the upper deck in ship-shape condition—scrubbing, cleaning, and painting it.

The Seaman Division contained three 'fighting' subdivisions, or branches, depending on who you asked: Gunnery, TAS (torpedo, anti-submarine) and RP (radar plotter). If you were thick you became a Gunner. Moderately thick, TAS. No thickness detected, RP. So, unsurprisingly, I became a Gunner. Surprisingly, so did Bomber.

Our final Saturday in the Annexe consisted of a properly folded, named, and clean kit muster. We stood nervously by our laid out kit as the DO, accompanied by Teresa, sought to find fault with anything and everything.

My turn.

'Does this rating have a problem with his name, POI Green?'

'He did have, sir. He's not the brightest rating I've come across.'

'Quite, but it's a reasonable muster.'

'Is that a pass, sir?'

'Yes, just, let's move on.'

I wasn't asked anything: none of Tiger mess was spoken to until the DO, having finished with our kit turned and addressed us all: 'A reasonable turn out, lads, but only reasonable. You'll find life much harder in the main establishment if you don't improve or want to improve. Carry on, POI.'

'Thank you, sir.'

As the DO left and moved on to the mess next door, Teresa gave his own opinion, told us to stow our kit properly in our locker, and to 'get this mess looking clean and tidy!'

We'd all passed kit muster! Relief fuelled our boisterous behaviour as we scrubbed, polished, and tidied Tiger mess for the last time.

Sunday saw us busy getting ready to leave the Annexe and join *Ganges proper*. After divisions, and avoiding any punishment, we stowed most of our kit in our kit bag, leaving out what we'd need to get us through to Monday morning. Our sewn-in-name No. 8s were re-ironed, boots polished, and hats scrubbed, ready for our march into the main establishment. After dinner we mostly slept through the demise of the Graf

44

Spee, then lazed on beds acting like old hands who'd been sailors forever.

We were soon brought back to reality. 'What's all this, then, what's all this!' shouted Teresa, making his presence known. 'I hope you're all ready for tomorrow, well, are you?'

'Yes, sir,' we responded, as one voice.

Teresa held up a piece of paper. 'This, this is a list of names and what class and mess you'll be in tomorrow when you join *Ganges proper*. Thought I'd leave it 'till now, didn't want you getting over-excited. And I've brought these labels. Make sure your name, class, and mess are written on three of em, three of em: one for your kit bag, one for your holdall, and the other for your ditty box. And after tea make sure this mess of a mess is tidied before I make my first rounds this evening: I'm the duty POI. Well... get on with it, get on with it!'

'Hey, Bomber, we're in the same mess and class.'

'Means I've to be looking after you again.'

'Yeah, and Kinky and Reedy and Paddy...'

'Looks like most of us are moving to the same mess. Best get these labels sorted, and, Lofty...'

'What?'

'Make sure yer spell yer name right.'

'Sod off, Bomber.'

Ganges (proper)

September 9th 1968

Main Gate

After breakfast we fell-in on the parade ground and were arranged into our *Ganges proper* messes. Bomber and I were to be in Keppel No.1 mess and in 41 class. The lads from another Annexe mess swelled our number to about forty.

We then had a practise march around the parade ground, ending with each mess being placed in marching order for entering *Ganges proper*. With Keppel No.1 mess being at the very top of the Long Covered Way, we took up the rear of the marching order: we were the last mess to be dropped off, so to speak.

For the first and last time we marched out of the Annexe main gate, down Bristol Hill, left onto Caledonia Road before the post office, and through the main gate of HMS Ganges.

For the first time in four weeks I saw ordinary people doing ordinary things. Some stopped what they were doing and stared, but most didn't—obviously used to ranks of Junior Ratings obstructing their main-road traffic.

Through the gates we passed the enormous parade ground and very tall mast on our left, and then double marched across the Quarter Deck.

After a long marching tour of Ganges *proper,* Teresa finally halted us at the top of the Long Covered Way, turned us right and stood us at ease. He nodded a 'they're yours now' towards two imposing POI's standing in front of our Keppel mess double-doors.

Teresa then marched himself away without any encouraging parting words, a cheery wave, or a dabbing of the corner of a tear-filled eye with a handkerchief.

Our kit bags, holdalls, and ditty boxes had been delivered and we carried them into Keppel No.1 mess. Keppel 41 class (Gunners) had the right-hand side, class 40 (TAS) the left. Bomber commandeered three beds in the middle of the line for himself, me and Kinky. His thinking, I learnt later, was that to include Kinky into our friendship bosom was to include somebody with a bit of inside knowledge, even though Kinky could be as irritating as nettles in your under crackers.

Keppel No.1 mess was similar to Tiger mess but much larger. The green and magnolia coloured walls, judging by the smell and cleanliness, had obviously been painted during summer leave, and the wooden deck held a shiny sheen. And, of course, just inside the mess and dead centre were the never-to-be-used dustbin and two never-to-be-used spittoons.

Two POI's introduced themselves as we stood at attention at the foot of our bed. Keppel 41 class had a Petty Officer Gunner named Case (known as Justin to us, obviously). The Keppel 40

47

class instructor, named Beech, sported a TAS badge on his right arm. His nickname was originally Nutty, but was soon replaced with Smiler because of his permanent scowl and lack of humour.

The two then took turns to explain their expectations, the mess rules, the rules when moving in and around Ganges, consequences if broken, the Ganges routine, and a brief summary of what we would be learning during this first Ganges term—a term that stretched all the way to Christmas leave.

Upon hearing footsteps the two POI's turned and saluted the Keppel Divisional Officer as he entered the mess: a tall, stout lieutenant with a nose like Rudolph's. He extolled the virtues of hard work, resolve in the face of adversity, self-discipline, good behaviour, the importance of keeping ourselves, our kit, and our mess clean, and to be proud when we left here as Ganges-trained Junior ratings.

Then came the realisation that life wouldn't get any easier in *Ganges proper*: 'You have a lot to do,' said our new DO, 'and until it's done you won't have any spare time. So no loafing about in the NAAFI, on the sports field, down on the foreshore, or anywhere else. This mess, especially the deck and, by the look of you, your kit, needs to be brought up to Ganges standard. You have until Saturday rounds to put this mess and yourselves in order. I want to see a vast improvement come Saturday, a vast improvement. Carry on, Petty Officers.' The DO returned the POI's salute and left the mess.

'STAND ATTA-EASE!' shouted Smiler. 'You have but an hour to properly stow your kit and make your bed. I don't want to hear any noise whilst you're about it. Do you, POI Case?'

'If I do, they'll get to know the parade ground quicker than they thought. Stop your gawping and get on with it!'

My locker seemed to be bigger than the one in Tiger mess but it still looked full after I'd stowed my kit. Where would I put the kit I hadn't been issued with yet? The finishing touch was draping a clean towel over a locker door, and I wondered why Ganges lockers had doors—they were never closed.

With kit stowed and beds made we fell-in under the colonnade outside our mess. Smiler marched us to the Central Mess Galley; a much larger version of the Annexe dining hall. Nicknamed 'The Screamer', this is where we would be fed and watered during our time at Ganges.

The nickname, apparently, came from the custom of tying splayed out obnoxious trainee chef nozzers to table legs and turning the lights off. In the dark would have been bad enough, but the CMG was a breeding ground for cockroaches, and the screaming would commence as they came out of their hiding places and invaded the poor nozzers clothing and orifices. Bomber said that it couldn't be true, nobody, even in Ganges, would do that to a nozzer. However, some years later, I would witness the exact same punishment being meted out to a particularly obnoxious Junior Stoker on board HMS Gurkha.

The food and choices were as good as in the Annexe. The only bugbear was queuing: with over 2000 boys to feed, queuing for long periods of time was irksome, but inevitable.

After dinner we only had a few minutes left before we were due back in the mess, so a few of us stopped for a quick smoke, making sure it was a Ganges-legal smoking area. Justin and Smiler were waiting for us outside Keppel 1, but it was Smiler who introduced us to the delights of mess cleaning—*Ganges proper* style.

'Fall in, quickly, fall in! Oh you lucky nozzers.' Lucky? Had we won a prize of some kind? Where we being sent home to review our career choice and to stay there if we deemed the choice a bad one? One can dream.

'All the walls have been freshly painted,' continued Smiler, 'so that only leaves the decks to smarten up. Lucky you, lucky you. Half of Keppel 40 will clean the heads, shower room, bathroom, and drying room decks. The rest of you will start to get your messdeck clean and polished. Gleaming, it will be gleaming in time for next Saturday rounds—or else!'

It wouldn't take that long, surely. But it did.

'Now, double quick, double quick!' shouted Smiler (he must have access to Teresa's parrot) 'change into your overalls and blue plimsolls then fall-in back here, double quick, at the double!'

Messdeck maintenance

Armed with sweeping brushes, dustpans, wire wool, cloths, scrubbing brushes, and buckets of hot soapy water, we nozzers cleaning the mess deck were led in by Justin.

The first task was to move beds and lockers from the right-hand side over to the left, exposing a third of needing-to-be cleaned and polished deck. Justin ordered us into groups of five. The 'sweeper' group commenced sweeping the deck from top to bottom, followed by the 'wire woolers' who, on hands and knees, scoured the deck, ridding it of the most recent layer of polish. Then the 'scrubbers' scrubbed the deck with hot soapy water, and the 'moppers-up' cleaned and rinsed, cleaned and rinsed.

Those not cleaning and rinsing replenished the buckets with clean, hot water and started moving beds and lockers to their rightful place. Then the beds and lockers from the left-hand side were moved over and the whole process began again.

We stopped for tea at about 17:00 hours, joining other overall-clad junior ratings in the CMG queue. Apparently, this deck cleaning was a start-of–the-term Ganges practice—not reserved for the newly arrived—so on this one occasion overalls were an allowed dress in the CMG.

Work stopped at about 20:00 hours after the left-hand side beds and lockers had been moved back. Showered and wearing pyjamas, we made our bed and sat on it, feet touching the floor. Justin came in through the mess door and instinctively we all stood to attention.

'At ease, sit down, you've earned a rest,' said Justin as he pinned a sheet of paper to the notice board.

'Tomorrow,' continued Justin 'is when you start training proper. On the board are your daily orders which tell you what you'll be doing, where and when. Call the hands is at 06:00 hours. Before that pipe is even finished you should be making your bed— properly. And I strongly suggest that you spend the time before breakfast making sure your working dress (No. 8s) are ironed and your caps, boots, and gaiters are all clean and shiny. After school tomorrow you'll be cleaning the middle of the deck. Read the orders, turn in—and no noise!'

'Hey, Kinky,' said Bomber, from the comfort of his bed.
'What?'
'Keep close to me and Lofty when we go into that seamanship place tomorrer.'
'Depends, Bomber, depends like.'
'Depends on what?'
'What's on offer is what.'
'A fag do?'
'Yeah, one from each of you, mind.'
'Lofty, did you hear that?'
'I'm out of fags, Bomber, and we aint allowed near the NAAFI.'
'Gimme three bob and I'll sort it.'
'Two bob!'
'Nice try, Lofty. Three bob or sod all.'

Turns out Bomber had met a Townie (a mate from his home town) in the CMG. He was in Blake division and a nearly-finished Ganges trainee. So after breakfast I got a packet of Kensitas for my three bob. Not cheap, but welcome.

At 07:30 Keppel 41 class mustered on the colonnade outside the mess. Justin marched us down to the foreshore where most of the training blocks where.

The inside of the Seamanship block was full of, well, seamanshippy stuff: from blocks and tackles to all sizes and lengths of rope. There were even mock-ups of ships showing how, amongst others, to anchor, to rig for replenishment at sea, and lower and raise a ship's boat.

But by far my most favourite room was the rope room. Here we learnt how to tie knots, make bends and hitches, whip rope ends, and splice them. Kinky, having been a Sea Cadet, already had some experience of knot tying, and it came to me fairly quickly, so we both helped a ham-fisted Bomber.

I didn't expect a single fag from Bomber for *my* services, and I wasn't disappointed.

Keppel 41 class September 1968

HMS Ganges had two routines: summer and winter. During the summer routine we had training and school throughout the day and sports during the early evening.

The winter routine differed in that sports took place in the afternoons, and we went to training or school in the early evening, obviously taking advantage of the limited daylight hours.

Milk was the stand-easy delight in summer; replaced by kye in winter.

After lunch we were marched to the grandiose-looking school. Here we would be taught maths, English, science, basic navigation, and naval history. The tuition culminated with taking the Navy, Army maths and English test (NAMET). Passing the test would enable progression to the rank of Leading Rate. But wanting to progress to Leading Rate or not, ratings had to pass this test before leaving Ganges.

The school instructors were more polite and softly spoken compared to the training instructors, which was a welcome relief. We sat at tables in a calm and relaxed atmosphere—not permanently at a state of attention-readiness.

After tea Keppel 1 completed the final third of messdeck cleaning—or so we thought.

We stood at attention as Smiler strolled up and down the mess inspecting our hard work. 'Good enough for polishing, do you think, Petty Officer Case?'

'I think so, we'll find out tomorrow.'

'Tomorrow, yes tomorrow.' He turned his attention to us. 'The rest of the evening is yours so make good use of the time. I can see a lot of untidy lockers and dirty boots. Do I have to say more? Make sure you're all turned in by 21:00.'

After the two POI's had left and it was safe to speak, a member of 40 class asked: 'Why turned in at nine? Lights out aint till half past.'

One of his class mates replied, 'That's so he can come back and read us a bed-time story!'

We all laughed then got stuck in to cleaning boots and tidying lockers that didn't really need any more tidying.

Tucked up in the soothing confines of my bed, I turned to Bomber, 'I hope they put everything back where it came from when they've finished polishing the deck.'

Bomber laughed, 'And I suppose you think we'll be having a whip-round for the window cleaner.'

Kinky joined in: 'Yeah, well, I'm still waiting for the boot-cleaning fairy.'

'Don't be daft...' The penny dropped. 'Sod off!'

Feeling, justly, like a fool my thoughts turned to the rope-work training we'd done that morning. Wanting to increase my knowledge I opened my Admiralty Manual of Seamanship (1964 Volume 1), turned to page 154 and endeavoured to learn more about *Bends and Hitches and General Rope Work.*

We didn't get to hear call the hands coming through the tannoys the next morning because Smiler was busy kicking the dustbin and shouting. I woke up wondering why Smiler was telling us the old 'where do policemen live' joke.

'Let's be aving you, let's be aving you!' Smiler shouted. 'Last nozzer out of his pit will be first nozzer cleaning the heads!'

After breakfast we mustered outside our mess on the Long Covered Way—a long, timber covered-in walkway that sloped down to the foreshore and admitted entry into about twenty messes and a few Divisional offices. Unfortunately, for obvious reasons, Keppel 1 mess's main door was opposite those few offices.

Morning Divisions was about to happen and we, excused from this daily ritual for now, were marched to the far side of the parade ground to witness the ceremony of colours: raising the white ensign on Ganges' huge mast. It was the same as Divisions we'd endured at the Annexe but on a much larger scale. We noted, with some degree of comfort, that even seasoned juniors were required to 'go round again'.

We'd been excused, Justin informed us, because looking and marching as we did now was a recipe for a Divisions disaster. However, he and Smiler had kindly arranged for our free time to be devoted to addressing those issues.

Marvellous—bloody marvellous.

School was as relaxed as it would always be and, after dinner, down in the Seamanship block, we continued with

General Rope Work. After tea my fantasy floor polishers proved to be just that—a fantasy.

Once again we moved the mess furniture to expose deck that was not up to Ganges shiny-deck standard. Once the deck had been cleaned, again with damp cloths, the shiny bit began

A line of juniors, on hands and knees, applied the thick, brown polish in a circular fashion using cloths. The next line worked the polish in using cloths wrapped around fist-sized wooden blocks. The next line, armed with the softer of our two boot brushes, buffed the deck to a reasonable shine. The next line, armed with clean, dry cloths brought the deck to what we thought was an acceptable Ganges shine.

We'd completed all three sections of the deck and were feeling very happy and proud of our hard work. Until...

'Call this a shiny deck!' shouted Smiler as we stood admiring our handiwork. 'This walkway,' he pointed to then strode down the middle of the mess, 'has to be gleaming! It's what the DO will see first as he comes in—can't bleeding well miss it can he? So it has to be so shiny that the DO will be forced to put his super-thick sunglasses on! All of you, all of you, grab your boot brushes and get this deck looking like I could shave myself in it!'

The Ganges ritual of buffing the middle of the deck with boot brushes every evening before we turned in, continued up until the last few weeks before we left.

Juniors mess

Swimming Test

'Hey, Lofty.'

'What?'

'You read Daily Orders?'

'Course I have.'

'Can you swim?'

'Like a fish, Bomber, like a fish. Can you?'

'I can float.'

'That's a start, I suppose.'

Kinky laughed. 'Hope they've hidden all the harpoons!'

'Cheeky sod.'

Kinky continued with his crap whale jokes: 'Stop blubbering, I need some kip. Blubbering—get it?'

'You'll be trying to swim with yer bed round yer neck...'

'Sod off you two...sod off!'

On most Saturday mornings during the summer, the youngest of the Neylan clan would catch a bus— or spend the bus fare on pop and sweets and walk into town—to spend most of the day in the 'Old Swimming Baths' (now a supermarket). The 'New Baths'—built in the forties!—were on the other side of town. Consequently I was a very good swimmer, even holding some lifesaving certificates and badges I'd earned at school. So the next morning held no trepidations for me as, dressed in white sports gear, carrying a towel and trunks, both classes double-marched to the pool.

The PTI's (Physical Training Instructors), who we had to address as 'I', not SIR (very confusing) didn't bother with asking who could swim and who couldn't. They found that out by having us all jump in at the deep end and swim to the shallow end.

Those who surfaced after the jump and immediately made for the side were pushed away by PTI's armed with long poles. The four who grabbed the poles and wouldn't let go were hauled out and made to stand, in shame, at attention, at the side. Bomber managed to float his way to the shallow end—but he didn't get away with the next test.

For the next part we donned overalls and swam to the deep end, trod water for three minutes then swam back. I say we, but Bomber didn't even make it out of the shallow end—he joined the ranks of non-swimmers. I was really enjoying this: I was in my element. And the enjoyment continued as we jumped off the top diving board, still wearing overalls.

After the test we competed against each other using front crawl and breast stroke. I was amazed when a PTI told me I'd very nearly matched the Ganges record for the 25 yards front crawl. He told me to 'get organised' (a favourite Navy expression) and join Keppel division swimming team. That didn't happen as I later chose dingy sailing as my representative sport.

Getting changed proved to be eventful when Kinky ended up on his backside after asking Bomber if he'd had a whale of a time.

An hour before call the hands came piping through the tannoys, or Smiler made his noisy appearance, the non-swimmers were dragged out of bed, double marched to the swimming pool and given extra swimming tuition. They had two weeks to achieve the required Navy standard. If they didn't they were classed as sinking ship liabilities and dismissed from the service.

Some, it has to be said, deliberately strove to be sinking ship liabilities so they could return home and choose a more convivial career. Bomber, somehow, achieved the required standard.

Having changed into No. 8s it was time to get paid. Nelson Hall was a huge hanger-type building that occupied most of the rear end of the parade ground, opposite the mast. Today it was occupied by pay-roll personnel sitting behind wooden tables.

We joined the Keppel queue in Ships Book number order, arranged by a very loud Chief Petty Officer Instructor. Once in front of the table I saluted, stated my name and ships book number, held out my left hand, received my pay, and saluted again as a thank you to the Navy for being paid.

This was to be my first and only pay parade. From then on my 'pocket money' would be paid directly into a Post Office Savings Bank.

My pay

Weekly pay:

7 days pay at 9shillings and sixpence = £3. 8s 3D
Kit Upkeep allowance =   -   9s 3D

Total   £3 17s 6D

Debits   National Insurance   - 9s 3D
Pocket money   £2 0s 0D
Cinema   - 1s 3D
Laundry   - 3s 3D
Recreation charge   - - 6D
Tailor/Cobbler/ Photographer   - 3s 6D

Total   £2 17s 9D

Why we paid so much for laundry when we had to do most of it ourselves, apart from sheets and blankets, was a mystery. Also a mystery was paying for the cinema even if we didn't go, and paying for the Tailor, Cobbler, and Photographer no matter how much we used them.

The major problem with money being paid into the POSB was having to queue at the village Post Office to withdraw any money we wanted or needed. This was restricted to a withdrawal of just a pound or so, depending on how much was in the account. Imagine the queues of about 2000 skint junior ratings wanting their pocket money. And we had to allow the local civilians to go to the front of the queue! Needless to say, on pension day we didn't bother at all.

The queues were alleviated somewhat when the Post Office woman opened a little office in the Admin building on certain afternoons. But the queues were still long and waiting was still tedious and very tiresome.

Boat-work

The calm, hot summer weather continued into September and Keppel 41 class were grateful for it as we marched down to the foreshore jetties, which jutted out into the river Stour, for our first boat-work instruction.

Being the first class for instruction that morning meant we had to crank down the whalers and cutters that were raised high out of the water on their davits. This involved winding two wheels: one at stem and stern that lowered the boats into the water. Justin told us that we were lucky being the first class today. The last class would have to crank the boats back up which, obviously, was much harder.

Justin divided the class then led the first to be trained down into a cutter whilst the others watched and learnt.

Here we learnt how to toss oars, ship oars, give way together, and boat oars. That was complicated enough but then we had to pull starboard, back port, pull port, back starboard in order to turn the cutter in a circle on the imaginary sixpence.

We were then introduced to the 3-in-one whaler, a boat that was the mainstay of British warships. It was called the '3-in-one' because it could be rowed, sailed, and had a small engine.

POI's who were, mostly, based at the boat jetties made sure we became proficient with rowing and steering the whalers—being in charge of the tiller was very exciting!

During our stand-easy, whilst we had our milk and a sticky bun, those ever delightful POI's tied a dustbin to the stern of our whaler. Rowing a whaler was a strain on the muscles at the best of times, but dragging a dustbin made me aware of muscles I didn't know I had.

Justin marched a tired and exhausted class back to the main establishment via three flights of concrete steps known colloquially as 'Faith Hope and Charity'. These steps were a favourite amongst Ganges POI's for administering punishment. Justin decided that we should become acquainted with this punishment as a deterrent for any future bad behaviour.

'These bottom steps are Faith,' said Justin, at the start of his introduction. 'Getting to the top of Faith fills you with the confidence of reaching the top of Charity. Next is Hope, where you HOPE you'll reach the top of Charity. On reaching the top of Charity you'll be grateful for getting there!'

It didn't look all that difficult: three flights of steps? I'd been running up and down the stairs at home since I could run. I couldn't see any problem with marching to the top of these steps. I was wrong, so very wrong.

'Class, class Ho! Ready, ready, wait for it - double march!' We doubled up the three flights of steps and, breathing heavily, leg muscles aching, halted at the top.

The stairs at home were even and standardised. These steps were definitely not, and I'd never ran up and down the stairs at home wearing heavy boots and gaiters, so doubling back down meant being as sure-footed as a mountain goat.

We doubled up and down twice more and Justin, probably unwilling to spend his dinner hour supervising his class in Ganges' sick quarters, double marched us back to the mess, and then dismissed us to the CMG to queue for dinner.

School in the afternoon was a welcome chance to ease and rest aching muscles. With Keppel 1's messdeck now polished and shiny we were allowed a sporty late afternoon. Most of us chose cricket, mainly because whilst we were the batting side we could lay on the grass, have a crafty fag and just watch—do nothing, just watch. Bliss.

I turned in that evening and was so shattered I couldn't even be bothered to open my Manual of Seamanship.

Dreaded Kit Muster

Saturday Daily Orders read: 10:00 Morning Rounds followed by kit muster.

After breakfast Justin and Smiler allocated the various cleaning duties. Every area was to be scrubbed and polished. Even our part of the colonnade had to be sparkly clean by 09:30.

I joined Chalky, Reedy, Paddy and Alfie Dewer, detailed with cleaning the windows— inside and out. Justin handed us some sheets of old newspaper and, noticing our 'what?' expressions, assured us of their cleaning power. Surprisingly, for all of us, old newspapers lived up to the assurances given by Justin. I made a mental note of passing this cleaning tip on to my mother when, eventually, we were granted leave. But immediately decided against it—I didn't want to spend half my leave cleaning windows.

Bomber had been given the task of cleaning the dustbin and spittoons with Bluebell polish. I swear he held the lingering stench of Bluebell throughout his remaining time at Ganges.

The final act of cleaning was forming lines of six, one behind the other on hands and knees, and then polishing the centre of the messdeck with the softest of our boot brushes.

Having changed into our red-threaded-named No. 8s we mustered outside on the colonnade. We came to attention as Justin informed the Keppel Divisional Officer that Keppel 1 mess was ready for inspection. After what seemed like an age the DO emerged from the mess and faced us.

'A good effort, a good effort, but nowhere near Ganges standard,' the DO said. 'I'll be back for kit muster. For your sakes it'd better be an improvement on your mess inspection effort!'

The kit muster entailed laying out the contents of your locker onto your bed in a precise and uniformed manner, with footwear on the deck at the foot of the bed.

We stood at attention, each waiting his turn. We could hear the DO grumping and growling as he inspected kit after kit. We daren't look— 'eyes front' had been the last order and we disobeyed it at our peril!

I could hear Bomber blustering through his kit inspection, and out of the corner of my eye saw a pair of boots sail through the air, then heard them clang against the dustbin.

Good shot!

My turn.

'Junior Seaman Neylan, sir,' said Justin, introducing me to the DO.

'Are you getting used to life in the Royal Navy?' The DO didn't wait for an answer. 'Do you know why it is important for your kit to be clean, ironed, and folded correctly?'

'Yes, sir.'

'Well... would you like to tell me or is THAT TOO INCONVENIENT! GOD FORBID I SHOULD TAKE UP TOO MUCH OF YOUR VALUABLE TIME!'

'Being clean is very important with crew living close together... on ships... and the lockers aren't very big... on ships... and...'

'ENOUGH! POI Case, make sure this rating READS his Ships Book. Make sure all of your class READ the dammed book! Now let's have a look at his kit.'

The DO used a long, thin cane to turn over items, unfold then lift them for a better view.

'This white front, young man. Why do you think it has that name?'

'Because...'

'I'll tell you,' growled the DO, holding the offending item up close to my face. 'It's supposed to be WHITE! Another failure, PO, another failure. I'm wasting my bleedin time! Right, they won't be at Divisions tomorrow because they haven't got their blue suits yet. Am I right?'

'Yes, sir, blue suits will be here Monday.'

'About time,' he walked swiftly to the top of the mess, turned and shouted: 'No recreation time for this mess today or this evening. You'll ALL spend the time getting your kit ready and FIT FOR MUSTER! I'll be back after Divisions tomorrow. BE READY!'

After questioning our parentage, intelligence, and attitude, Justin and Smiler left us rectifying kit.

Kinky wasn't best pleased: 'Bleedin ell, I'd have passed if he'd got to me!'

'Put a sock in it, Kinky,' retorted Bomber. 'He knew he was going to fail us all before he bleedin started - miserable old sod.'

'Jeez,' I said, then proffered a Yorkshire term that supposedly justified bad temper: 'His dog must have died.'

Paddy Dooly chipped in, 'Yeah, well, his dog'll be where we are.'

'And where's that, Paddy?'

'In the dog house, so it will, in the bleedin dog house.'

'You're Irish, and that was that your best joke?'

'What was wrong with your boots, Bomber?'

'Same as your white front, Lofty—bugger all!'

Saturday and early Sunday morning (even our Sunday fifteen minute lie in was withdrawn) was spent preparing for our second kit muster. Most of us passed this time but two poor sods had their kit rolled in a blanket and dumped in the heads. We all thought this was over the top and cruel but, after all, this is Ganges: we were quickly learning not to be surprised by extreme punishment—but to expect it.

Vertigo Test

Monday morning found the weather continuing with its sunny warmth. Ideal conditions for undertaking the next you-must-pass-this-test in order to continue training at Ganges—climbing the mast.

After Divisions (we were now deemed competent enough to make a convincing contribution) we mustered on the Long Covered Way dressed in white sports kit, unexcitedly awaiting Justin's promise of an exciting morning. Justin prepared us for this assessment of our levels of vertigo tolerance by double marching us twice around the large parade ground, then bringing us to a halt before the mast, its imposing and impressive143 feet reaching up into the clear, blue sky.

Justin made his way to the rear of his emotionally mixed class: some were raring to go, some were not so raring and some, like me, had no raring in them at all. Justin was replaced by two bending and stretching PTI's, who invited us to join in with their bending and stretching exercises. It would have been foolhardy to refuse their invitation so we bent and stretched in preparation for the climb ahead.

The PTI's gave us a demonstration of how to get to the rigging and how to coordinate our limbs whilst climbing. One PTI then scrambled up the ratlines (a series of light lines tied across the shrouds, used for climbing aloft) and stopped just under the Devil's Elbow, about sixty feet up from the parade ground. This was a wooden platform that was accessed by either climbing up through one of two Lubbers Holes, or swinging out and climbing ratlines whilst leaning out from the mast at a forty degree angle.

The climbing PTI, choosing the latter option, leaned out and climbed aloft. Reaching the platform he pulled himself up and over and stood looking down at a class of very anxious faces.

'See,' bellowed the grounded PTI, 'see how easy that was!'

Easy? That PTI had been dangling in fresh air! I can't do that, I said to myself, then thinking how I could possibly remove the inevitable stains from my Navy-issued underwear before the next kit inspection.

'Now,' continued PTI terra firma, 'because the Navy, in my opinion, has gone soft, you lot have only to reach the Devil's Elbow, AND!' he shook his head in exasperation, 'you're allowed to get there by using the Lubbers Hole! The Lubbers Hole, the ruddy Lubbers Hole!'

The air-born PTI, for demonstration purposes, climbed down through a Lubbers Hole, accompanied by an audible gasp of relief from the vertigo affected.

Phew, at least I could now keep upright: I wasn't about to dangle in mid air with my back to the deck—Lubbers Hole for me!

'I'm not soft,' whispered Reedy, 'I'm going up and round.'

'Then you're soft in the heed,' muttered Paddy, 'so you are.'

'Lubbers Hole for me,' whispered Chalky: 'I'm a coward, on me dad's side.'

'Quiet there, quiet, less of the ruddy noise!' shouted PTI terra firma. 'Down! Ten press ups!' After ten press ups. 'Ten sit ups! Now—NOW!'

Jeez, why was he weakening muscles our lives would soon become dependent on?

'First three, take your place and prepare to go aloft! Don't hang around admiring the view—and the nervy types—don't look down! And if you do fall off the rigging, the safety net will keep you from hurting your miserable, pathetic bodies.'

Crikey, if Bomber fell from up there he'd hit the net and become a horrible mass of human waiting-to-be-fried chips beneath it.

'I suppose you've heard about the young lad who fell, bounced on the net and died when he went through the Post Office roof. Well, don't worry; none of you will get up as far as he was when he fell.'

No, we hadn't heard, but quietly thanked him for his warped reassurance.

Suffice to say we all managed to pass the mast test, most via the Lubbers Hole. And, just under the Devil's Elbow, Reedy changed his texture from hard to soft, bravely accepting all derisory comments.

Why were we made to climb the mast when there was more chance of being drilled by a CGI who didn't shout, than any chance of getting drafted to a Royal Navy sailing ship? Discipline: all part of the imbedding of carrying out orders, immediately, without question, an unfailing obedience. That was the reason—that was the Ganges way.

In my opinion there has never been a more impressive sight than witnessing the ceremonial manning of the mast by juniors at HMS Ganges.

Devil's Elbow and Lubbers Hole(s)

Justin chose not to comment on our mast climbing and marched us to the slop room where we were to take possession of our first, much anticipated, blue serge uniform.

*There are conflicting stories regarding the rating that fell from the mast. I'm only repeating what we were told.

The 'blue serge uniform' was a basic jacket and bell-bottom trousers affair. However, it came with attachments that required folding, tying, and ironing in strict, complicated ways. This first issue was our No. 2s general wear uniform, usually accompanied with boots and gaiters, and any badges sewn onto its arms would be red in colour.

By contrast our No.1 uniform was made with fine wool and usually worn with shoes, except for ceremonial occasions when boots, white gaiters and belt would be worn, and any badges sewn on would be gold in colour. We didn't get our No.1s until we became Junior Seaman (first class) towards the end of our Ganges training.

The most complicated part of both versions of our uniforms was the ironing of the bell-bottom trousers. They had to be ironed with horizontal, concertinaed creases, with a spacing of 3 1/2 inches. My taller mess mates, who took the mick out of my height (or lack of it), had to have seven creases. So being a shortie had its benefits: at less than 5 feet 8 inches tall, I only had five creases to iron.

The 'Guard Duty' photograph shows winter dress (obviously), when we wore a prickly, itchy sea jersey instead of a white front. Some lucky beggars had their mum sew a nice, comfy cotton lining inside their jerseys. They were not only itchy free, but considerably warmer!

However the owning and wearing of a proper sailors uniform led to conflicting emotions: we now had to participate fully in Sunday morning divisions, but we could now go (as limited as it was) on shore leave.

Boxing

The following week saw us undertaking the final physically challenging you-must-pass-this-test in order to continue training at Ganges—boxing!

Daily orders stated that immediately after divisions all of our recruitment were to change into blue sports kit and be ready to take part in a boxing tournament.

'Now's your chance to show the spirit you've all been lacking so far,' shouted Smiler as we were changing. 'Now's your chance to knock seven bells out of each other—legally!'

'You'll be knocking seven bells out of some sods knee caps, Lofty,' whispered Bomber.

'Yeah, Lofty,' Kinky whispered, darting a look to see if Smiler could see his lips moving, 'start at his shins and work your way up.'

There was muffled laughter from those within hearing range. But I wasn't rising to the bait. In fact, I was quite looking forward to a bit of a legal scrap. I had three brothers and we would fight all the time. At the school I went to, and in the area where I lived, there was always somebody spoiling for a fight. And I'd had my share; winning some and losing some. Backing down or running away from a fight was never an option—that would send the wrong message to all the local bullies.

Suitably dressed for boxing we mustered outside on the Long Covered way. As usual, we were inspected, shouted at and told that any blood stained clothing was to be washed immediately upon our return. Then we double marched to the large gymnasium.

Once inside we were seated in mess groups to three sides of the elevated, newly erected boxing ring. The remaining side was occupied by the recruitment that had just about finished their training, and off duty Ganges ships company ratings who were obviously devotees of blood and gore horror films.'

A massively built PTI stood in the centre of the ring. He had a bent nose, cauliflower ears and, surprisingly, a very high-pitched voice.

'Welcome, one and all, to this latest recruitments boxing tournament.' He then directed his attention to our mixed group of eager and reluctant combatants. 'To make each fight fair, you lads have all been paired off according to your weight. All the rules of boxing will be adhered to. You should all know the rules so we won't waste time with them.'

Which page of the Ships Book was boxing rules on, I wondered.

'When your name's called, climb into the ring and sit on a stool. There will be a PTI there to look after you... stop any bleeding... and all that. When the referee tells you to box, you BOX. You don't run away, surrender, or fall to the deck! Understood? Oh, there will be three rounds of two minutes continuous boxing, unless, of course, there's a knock out or life-threatening injuries occur. The first two boxers are...'

Two junior ratings climbed through the ropes, sat on a stool, had their gloves fitted, then joined the referee in the middle of the ring. The ref had a few words with the opponents—his words drowned out by shouts of encouragement and advice as to how best maim or disfigure each other.

'BOX', shouted the ref and the two boxers charged at each other. One of them was throwing punches before he'd even reached his opponent—his eyes firmly closed. So he didn't see the jab that slipped between his flailing gloves and flattened his nose. He staggered back—luckily avoiding a swinging right hook—with blood spurting from his damaged nose. The ref, carefully dodging the spurting blood, dived between the boxers, looked into the eyes of the damaged one, gave a grunt and, despite the crowd baying for more, reluctantly declared him unfit to continue.

Bomber's turn came. His opponent was of a similar build, so it looked as if it was going to be a good, long fight. Bomber, however, had other ideas. I must admit to being a little dismayed as Bomber just stood there, gloves up, as his opponent, obviously pleased with Bomber's lack of aggression, hit him with a flurry of blows to his body and arms.

'Fight, fight, fight!' bayed the blood-thirsty crowd. But Bomber stood his ground, absorbing blow after blow. Just before the ref intervened to vent his displeasure at Bomber's lack of fighting spirit, Bomber's adversary ran out of steam. As his tired arms dropped, Bomber *dropped* him with a hay-maker of a punch to his left temple. I do believe he was out before his crumpled frame hit the canvas.

'You crafty sod,' I said to a grinning Bomber as he regained his place on the bench.

'Yeah, worked dinnit, but don't you be doing the same, Lofty... you're not exactly built for it, sure yer not.'

'You must have had a right clout on your head, Bomber: all of a sudden you've got an Irish accent.'

'To be sure, Lofty... to be sure.'

My turn.

I climbed through the ropes, sat on a corner stool and had my gloves laced by the PTI. Over in the opposite corner was a rating who must have been over six feet tall, not as far through as a pipe cleaner, and with skin whiter than a PTI's vest.

My corner PTI saw me looking: 'Don't worry, son, the bigger they are, the harder they fall.' Now where had I heard that nonsense before?

I faced my opponent in the middle of the ring as the ref enlightened us with the do's and don'ts. The cocky white bean pole was grinning from ear to ear, obviously relishing in his height advantage and looking forward to knocking seven bells out of my small frame.

'Box!' shouted the ref. My ears were filled with cries of 'bite his ankles, give him a ladder!' and similar. The baiting fuelled my aggression and I resolved to give a good account of myself. Then I got lucky: the confident bean pole pulled his right arm back and sprang forward, ready to deliver his knockout punch. Big mistake: he left his midriff wide open, which gave me the opportunity to step in close and hit him as hard as I could with a left hand jab to his belly button. My luck was growing: winded, he dropped his arms, and as he doubled-up my right glove met his falling chin.

Next thing I know the ref is raising my left glove and declaring me the winner! I felt proud of myself as, with the cheers of Keppel Division ringing in my ears, I returned to my place on the bench.

'Bloody hell,' said Kinky, 'you're a bit of a dark horse.'

Bomber just smiled.

Despite Keppel Divisions two knockouts, it was Grenville Division who had the most wins, and therefore declared the tournament winners.

Mutiny on Laundry Hill

Once a week we had an allotted time to make use of Ganges' laundry. We still used the sinks in the washroom to wash our smalls and hang them in the drying room, or outside on washing lines strung up in the space between messes, but all other items had to be taken to the laundry.

On this particular week, taking our cue from daily orders, we dutifully, at the time stated, dressed in blue sports kit, took the sheet we'd used as the bottom one from our neatly piled bedding and heaped all our dirty kit onto it, along with our newly acquired cleaning aid—dhobi-dust (washing powder) which we bought from the NAAFI shop. Dhobi is Hindi for washing. How it came to be included in Royal Navy slang is a complete mystery.

Having double marched to the laundry with the sheet full of washing slung over our left shoulder, we fell-out and removed our plimsolls, leaving them in neat rows outside.

Inside were huge, cylindrical washing machines, but we didn't completely escape hand washing—every item with a collar had to have its collar scrubbed, using liberal doses of dhobi-dust, before it could be placed in a washing machine. The dust was far better than pussers hard for removing sweat and muck, and the resulting soap suds were somehow reassuring—and it smelled better!

Once the machines had finished their contribution to the Ganges cleanliness regime, we hung everything on racks in the huge drying room. Unfortunately for us our laundry time slot this week was in the afternoon, so we'd have to be up and out of our pits a half-hour before call the hands the next morning to come and collect our dried dhobiing.

But far worse than the earlier rise and shine was to find that someone, probably one of those-soon-to-be-released-after-finishing-their-training nozzers—or, Smiler, as many of us later suspected—had strewn our neatly placed plimsolls up and down the whole length of Laundry Hill whilst we'd been laundering.

'Well, well, well,' beamed Smiler, delighted with the prospect of inflicting unwarranted punishment. Justin shook his head in an 'I know what's coming next' manner as Smiler deviously twisted unwarranted into warranted.

'You didn't leave a guard, a guard to watch over your kit!' he shouted.

We all stared uncomprehendingly, eyes front.

'Would you, would you, as a landing party on some foreign shore, landed to fight enemies of our Queen and country, leave your kit, weapons, and ammunition unguarded whilst you set up camp or stopped for a stand-easy? NO YOU RUDDY WOULD NOT!' What the... 'Fall-out, pick up your plimsolls, put them on and fall back in—NOW!'

Laundry Hill, often described as a long, gentle slope from the instruction block down to the running track, was anything but gentle when doubling up and down it. Indeed, some years before, a rating had collapsed and died after a zealous and pitiless POI had used the hill to inflict excessive punishment on his class. The Ganges reaction was to limit the doubling time to a maximum of ten minutes. How thoughtful.

We were, by now, used to the torment of Faith Hope and Charity, but this was worse, far worse. The long, 'gentle' slope inflicted pain on every leg joint and muscle, with breathing becoming more and more difficult as we pounded up the hill. Going down didn't bring the expected respite—stomping hard to avoid a stampede put more strain on already strained muscles. And there was also the mental agony of knowing we'd have to about turn at the bottom and double back up.

During our third ascent, I think, some poor sod from Keppel 40 class decided enough was enough. He broke ranks, stumbled over the kerb and lay sprawled on the grass verge.

'Mess halt!' bellowed Smiler. We came to a halt, relieved at the unexpected respite. 'GET UP AND FALL BACK IN!' screamed Smiler at the prostrate figure.

'I can't, I'm done,' came the slurred reply.

'DONE! DONE! GET YOUR LAZY CARCASS OFF THE DECK, OFF THE DECK—NOW!'

'Sod off, Smiler, just sod off and leave me be.'

We all had enough breath left to release an audible gasp. Smiler, he'd called him Smiler—jeez, we deemed that worse than the 'sod off' part.

Smiler's face turned so red it could have stopped traffic. Standing over the would-be mutineer he raised his stick, preparing to make matters worse. Justin, obviously recalling what a similar incident had led to, introduced some common sense to the drama. He walked over to Smiler, had a word in his ear then detailed three ratings at the front of the column to help him get the exhausted rebel to the sick bay.

Smiler double marched both classes back to the mess. On arrival he shouted like a petulant child: 'Don't you lot be thinking you can just fall down and give up, cos you can't!' With that warning he dismissed us to ready ourselves for tea.

The next afternoon, upon returning to the mess after a day of arduous learning, we noticed a stripped and empty bed amongst the ranks of 40 class. The brave mutineer had, we later learnt, been shipped home, no longer considered being trusted to uphold the Royal Navy's excellent reputation.

And so Ganges life continued: tuition, Parade drill, kit musters, inspections, expected punishment, and Divisions.

Sunday Divisions was a particularly taxing event. We wore shoes with our blue, No. 2 suit. And they had to be as shiny as mirrors from heel to toe—or else!

We were inspected by numerous nit-picking authoritative personnel, with any imperfection jotted down by Smiler and Justin into their notebooks; or, as we called them - punishment books.

Our overriding imperfection was the belief that we were all in need of a haircut—doubling round the parade ground was perceived as a way of a reminder.

After divisions we marched to God's Hill, where we were preached to in our designated-religion churches.

I say churches—I'd declared myself a Methodist when I'd signed on proper in the Annexe, so I was lumped in with the minority religion lot: Methodist, Presbyterian, Church of Scotland etc, collectively known as the Free Church.

Our church was merely a passing nod to God - a small but large enough room to accommodate a small congregation and a large crucifix.

We would sing a tuneless hymn then listen to a moralistic story. Fortunately we weren't considered to be worth saving, or the Preacher had better things to do (I suspected both), and after only fifteen minutes or so we were set free. This meant we were early to change and be amongst the first in the queue for Sunday dinner.

However, every month or so all Ganges personal received their religious blessings inside No.1 gymnasium. We sat on benches facing the front of the gym where, on each side of the facing wall, written in large letters, was the Rudyard Kipling poem 'IF'. If I could meet all the requirements stated in the poem, I'd become a man. An apt choice of a poem that fitted in nicely with the ideal of Ganges: turning boys into men.

The one and only thing I looked forward to at Sunday service in the gym was the singing of 'Eternal Father, Strong to Save' (a hymn commonly known as 'For those in peril on the sea').

Smashing!

The summer of 1968 finally lost its glory to bouts of rainfall as October drifted into November's winter routine. It was now the season of winter sports, dominated by rugby, football, and cross-country running.

I was okay with football and running, but rugby was only played in Grammar schools where I lived, so it was a new experience. Because of my small physique and inexperience, I'd spend most of every game running away from that strange-shaped ball.

It was also time to swap white fronts for sea jerseys. When I was at school it was a common, evil, practise to squeeze rose hips and sprinkle the ferociously itchy seeds down the back or front of unsuspecting victims clothing. Wearing a sea jersey, for me, felt like it was lined with rose hip seeds. I suffered—and suffered.

Assault Course

As November came to an end our main focus and topic of conversation was Christmas leave. We'd been in Ganges' cocooned grip for nigh on three months, and the thought of even a brief return to civvie street far outweighed troubled thoughts of kit musters, inspections, Parade drill etc, and all the punishments we'd have to endure for failure.

I was particularly looking forward to walking familiar streets and talking to people who I knew far better than anyone at Ganges. Also, I wasn't expecting to have to muster my kit for my mother, or have her inspect me before I went out, fearful that I might have to double up and down Cusworth hill if she found any faults.

However, before Christmas leave, a gleeful Justin informed us that 41 Class were overdue their introduction to the assault course.

Huddled near a radiator, a group of us were cleaning gaiters or spit-polishing boots.

'Have you seen that assault course?' said Sam, to no one in particular, 'looks like more bleedin fun.'

'Yeah, like, we've all seen it, must be blind if you haven't,' said Kinky, in between blowing hot breaths on a boot toe cap.

'Buggers could have waited 'till next summer,' said Alfie, 'it'll be bloody freezing.'

'I could hear em shouting and screaming from Laundry Hill,' said Paddy Dooly, 'and that's miles away.'

'Not miles...'

'A long bloody way, then, but I bet they'll hear Kinky screaming and complaining over in Harwich, so they will.'

'Cheeky sod...'

After tea Justin entered the mess and pinned next day's Daily Orders to the notice board.

'So you're prepared, and because I'm a kindly soul,' said Justin as we were sorting lockers and kit, getting ready for evening rounds, 'dress for the assault course, as-you-will-see, is overalls and blue plimsolls. Used to be blue sports kit but, despite the claims on your dhobi dust boxes, nozzers couldn't remove the assault course stains...'

'Soon, very soon,' interrupted Smiler, making his unwelcome appearance, 'the Ganges name above our beloved main gate will be changed to ruddy Butlins! You lot should be paying the Navy to be here—paying the Navy!'

'And to save your plimsolls,' continued Justin, 'some nozzers swear by giving them a rub with Vaseline.' I could envisage some lucky sod with a jar of Vaseline making a right killing. 'And wear an old vest; it's going to be cold, very cold.'

Old, old? We hadn't been here long enough for anything to be old. A sacrifice would have to be made.

'I hope, before you leave this fine establishment,' shouted Smiler, 'you reward POI Case for his kindness. Me? All I ask for is obedience, sweat, and tears!'

Nobody had any Vaseline and the NAAFI was closed until tomorrow morning, well after we'd started the assault course. But all was not lost: Reedy suggested we avoid stepping in the mud. I just hope he's not manning a help-line somewhere.

Dressed in overalls, a sacrificial vest and plimsolls (no socks), we doubled to the assault course. Smiler kept us doubling on the spot—to keep us warm—whilst we waited for the course staff to make an appearance.

Eventually a Chief Petty Officer PTI, followed by a horde of bending stretching PTI's, brought us to a halt. He was a big bloke, both upwards and outwards. I wondered if an increase in size automatically moved PTI's up the ranks. No, this PTI would have been an admiral.

'Welcome, my lads, welcome to an assault course designed by the Royal Marines! But they, even they, don't attempt it anymore since I, yes me, redesigned it after I was drafted here.'

Just get on with it; we're frightened enough without your lies were, I'm sure, the thoughts of us all.

'Because, because,' continued the giant, 'I'm all for having nozzers looking forward to a good time, I'll walk you through the course so you'll all know what a good time you're going to have! Single file, single file, follow me, follow me!'

Another parrot.

The first thing to conquer—apart from our fear—was a brick wall as tall as the CPTI and festooned with dangling, knotted rope. After that the challenges became, well, more challenging – ankle-high nets, covering ankle-deep mud to scramble under, sewer-sized pipes, a deep breath long, filled with green, slimy water to crawl through, and many aerial delights. To finish was a fifty-yard sprint carrying a lump of sodden wood.

Marvellous!

'Now, then, you sissies,' shouted the giant, after we'd returned to the start. 'You'll be sissies no more when you've made it back here. You have thirty minutes, yes, a whole half–hour to complete the course. A second over, just a second, and you'll be trying again on Sunday afternoon! I'm all for team work, team work is what keeps this Navy the best in the world. If you can help an oppo'—friend—' then do so. But, but, that's no excuse for running out of time—no excuse!'

The bending and stretching PTI's dispersed to their life-saving positions, and then we were off!

I managed to scramble over the wall, with help from the dangly ropes and a boot up the backside and, after what seemed like hours of crawling under nets, being hauled out of water filled pipes by the scruff of my neck, swinging between high platforms on ropes or crossing them cuddling a telegraph pole, I picked up a sodden log and staggered to the finishing line—I, like most of the others, hadn't the energy left for a brisk walk, never mind a sprint.

I wasn't last to finish: there were a few more behind me. Struggling at the rear, really struggling was Paddy Dooly. Two of the first back, Spud and Chalky, ran to his aid and helped him, and his log, over the line with just seconds to spare.

Team work—smashing!

'Not a bad effort considering it's your first time,' conceded the CPOI. 'But next time, next time, you'll do it in twenty minutes! Something for you to look forward to!'

But there wasn't a 'next time'. I don't know why but we didn't have to endure the assault course again. Only something the insane amongst the class regretted.

That evening, after pipe down, with overalls and blue plimsolls soaking in the washroom, and my sacrificial vest—which hadn't combated one iota of cold—in the bin, Kinky began his usual bravado act:

'Anybody up for another go at that course Sunday?'

Silence

'Come on, see if we can do it under the twenty minutes like.'

'Kinky,' said Spud, 'you were only just in front of Paddy...'

'Yeah, you were,' confirmed a few voices.

'That's cos I helped Chalky swing over that gap.'

'Helped me?' questioned Chalky. 'You only threw the bloody rope back! Then I went past you on that pole you were hugging.'

'Well, you go,' said Alfie, 'and tell us all about it Sunday night - fairy stories help me sleep.'

'Can't go on my own...'

'For Christ's sake, Tarzan, shut yer gob and leave us to get some sleep.'

'Hey, Lofty,' said Bomber, snuggling down into his bedding.

'What... don't tell me you're stupid enough to...'

'Not on yer nellie, no. Was thinking - if you get up to go to the heads during the night, like...'

'And...'

'Could you give me overalls a quick stir on yer way back?'

'Sod off, Bomber.'

Christmas 1968

The trains taking Ganges on leave left Ipswich very early in the morning at around 05:00. Daily orders stated that call the hands would sound at 02:00, breakfast at 02:30 pay parade in Nelson Hall at 03:30 then boarding coaches for the mass exodus to Ipswich railway station at 04:30.

In order that we would be bright-eyed and bushy-tailed the next morning, dinner today would be followed by all junior seaman packing their little holdalls before turning in at 14:00 .With all of us in holiday mode, excited by soon escaping the Ganges routine, the duty POI strode into the mess and restored normality.

'Too much noise, too much noise!' he shouted, 'if you don't want to be doubling round the parade ground on Christmas day instead of opening mummy's presents, I suggest you pipe down and keep it quiet—QUIET!'

'He's from Drake Division,' whispered Bomber after the POI had left. 'They reckon he's meaner than a scrap yard dog.'

'Yeah, well,' said Alfie, 'I don't want him biting my arse before I go home, so we'd best do as he says.'

Mindful of the duty POI's reputation, we turned in and forced ourselves to sleep.

The following morning, after a very early breakfast, and dressed in our blue suits, we searched ditty boxes looking for the only-once-used pay book, wondering what the pay parade was for.

'Well, I'm thinking,' said Reedy, 'the Captain's giving us a Christmas bonus as thanks for not deserting.'

'I think we might be getting a rebate cos of the crap films they put on,' said Chalky.

Justin strode into the mess and stopped our wondering: 'You'll be getting £15, yes, fifteen, fine English pounds - but it's not for you - it's a ration allowance to pay your parents for feeding, watering, and looking after you whilst you're away from your favourite place. And make sure they get it! Don't be spending it on wine, women, and song! You'll also be getting a train ticket, a return ticket—so don't be losing it!'

Luckily for us North East northerners, the train from Ipswich would travel all the way up to Newcastle, stopping to drop off ratings along the way.

I was surprised to be among three Ganges recruits who stepped off the train at Doncaster station. They seemed as surprised as me as we swapped names and information concerning the Division we were in, and where in Donny we lived.

We parted with reassurances that we'd keep an eye out for each other back at Ganges—having townie mates back in the rigours of Ganges was somehow comforting.

Having stocked up with fags at the station kiosk, and making sure my Burberry (overcoat) was securely folded between the handles of my holdall, I made my way to the North Bridge assembly of bus stops.

The Castle Hills double-decker wasn't full and I didn't see anyone I knew amongst the few passengers. As I walked down the aisle to get off at the top of Pipering Lane, a middle-aged lady asked if she could touch my collar - 'for luck, you know'. I do believe I blushed.

'Mam! our Chris' home,' shouted Steve, one of my two younger brothers, as I walked in through the back door.

'Well it's done you some good, that Navy place,' said my mam, appearing from the front room and looking me up and down. 'You've grown a few inches and you're not slouching like you used to.'

Thanks mam.

'I've made a stew for tea; I'll be putting it out soon.'

'I asked me mam to make you a stew cos I know you like it,' said my youngest sister, Pamela, who'd decided my cap looked far better on her than it did on me.

'You a proper sailor now, our Chris?' asked my youngest brother, Tim, stirring from his favourite place near the coal fire.

I answered as many questions as I could, skilfully avoiding the fact that I'd not actually seen any sea as yet.

I'd thought about having my tea then, still dressed in my uniform, going out to call on a few mates. But the sea jersey was devouring my flesh at a phenomenal rate, so I went upstairs to change, lastly slipping on my purple-hued boots - boots I'd saved up for and bought to impress Jimmy Duggan's sister. But, alas, she'd been more impressed with Charley Beresford's moped—and he was a year older than me.

When I came back down my mum wasn't best pleased: 'You could have left your uniform on so everybody could see you in it,' she said, taking the large pan of stew out of the coal oven.

'I'll put it on before I go back,' I replied. 'Look at what that jerseys done to my skin. Where's my dad? At his allotment?'

'You're soft as muck, always have been. He's on afters; be home just after 10.'

She sat beside me at the table and filled me in on recent family developments as I ate my stew.

Andrew had just started a job at H.L. Browns Jewellers on Doncaster High Street. Jane was working in the Pilgrim bookshop in town. Wendy was in Sheffield training to be a nurse and my oldest sister, Susan, was working in the offices at International Harvesters, and was still courting Brian, her eventual husband.

Brian had introduced me to the inspiring songs of Bob Dylan, and I was eager to find out if Bob had released a new LP—now known as albums (sigh).

I finished my stew, stood up and fished out £15 from a back pocket of my jeans. 'This is for you, mam. The Navy says you have to have it to pay for my food and all that.'

'Is that all the money you've got?'

'No, they put my pay into a post office book, and I've got a few bob in it.'

'Well, I never expected it, but it'll come in handy.'

With five of us now paying board, I thought she would have at least handed a fiver back.

But she didn't.

I went out and headed for my mate Walleys house. An only child, he lived in a big house on Jossey Lane, and his parents were happy for him to have lots of mates calling at once. I thought that's where a few of my mates would be.

As it happens there was quite a crowd in the big house's front room. I caught up on all the news, but soon realised that nothing much had changed, except that Charley Beresford had upgraded to a motorbike.

Sod it!

I was asked countless questions about Ganges, and became frustrated when my answers and explanations were met with bewilderment and disbelief; quickly realising you'd have to have been there to fully comprehend life at Ganges.

The three weeks leave flew by, and I awoke on the morning of my return to Ganges apprehensive and anxious.

I said my goodbyes to Tim, Steve, and Pamela—the only members of my family still in the house—then made my way to Doncaster train station. I wouldn't return to spend any future leave at home until after I'd joined my first sea-going ship.

Keep on keeping on...

1969

At the start of the spring term the junior rating count at Ganges, according to rumour, had been reduced.

Three ratings went absent without leave. Another one chopped a finger off, extending his leave with the hope of being medically discharged, and another was immediately discharged after punching a CPO on the nose at Ipswich station. Keppel 1 mess were all accounted for—it appeared that, compared to some POI's, Smiler wasn't that bad after all. But he still had us boot-brushing the middle of the deck before we turned in that first evening.

Normality was restored.

The winter weather in Suffolk that year was unusually cold and brutal - drizzle turned to Arc-building ferocious rain in an instant, with snow constantly battling for domination.

Just our luck, then, that 41 class moved to the top of the list for rifle range instruction.

I'm sure that most young boys in those days would have played Wild West and war games during their childhood. I certainly remember tying my youngest sister, Pamela, to the washing line pole in the back garden, then rescuing her in a blaze of gunfire.

So most were looking forward to shooting with a real gun. But it wasn't until we were seated in one of the range classrooms that we realised that shooting a gun wasn't going to be as easy as forming a pistol with a hand and shouting 'POW'.

The first hour was dedicated to a CGI showing us all the small-arms weapons available to the Royal Navy, their names, and where they may be best deployed. We were allowed to call him Chief, but only at the range. On the parade ground, make no mistake, he would be sir!

After stand-easy's welcome mug of hot kye (no fags; we'd been forced to leave all smoking paraphernalia in the mess), the chief focused on the SLR (Self Loading Rifle), the weapon we had to be most familiar with.

Issued with an SLR from the armoury, we handled (fondled) it, stripped it, cleaned it, put it back together then did it all over again—many times. We loaded the magazine with 7.62 ammunition (not bullets—ammunition or rounds—never bullets), unloaded it and loaded it—many times. To finish that morning's tuition we inserted the empty magazine, detached it, and inserted it, over and over again.

'Tomorrow morning,' bellowed the Chief, 'I just might, might, mind you, let you shoot with an SLR! Fall in outside!'

Justin was waiting for us. He turned us to the left and we double marched back to the mess to clean up and get ready to queue for dinner.

The next morning, in the range classroom we'd used yesterday, we were drilled in all things safety; particularly how to make sure the rifle was safe after finishing shooting. Then the inevitable rifle cleaning.

After the Chief had satisfied himself with our efforts he had us fall-in outside, armed with rifles. Knowing that we'd never experienced marching with a rifle, he let us amble down to the shooting range. Yes, Amble!

Facing us was a cliff of sand, lined half way down with cardboard cut outs of well-armed, life-sized ferocious-looking Eastern Bloc soldiers. I was amongst the first five detailed to take up a prone, shooting position, lying down on freezing and icy remnants of grass. But I wasn't there long. A huge hand gripped my collar and pulled me upright.

'What the bleedin 'ell are you doing there?' shouted the chief, his hot breath temporarily defrosting my left ear.

'You said to...'

'You're a ruddy left-hander!' He dragged me to the right-hand side of the prone group and flung me facedown onto an undisturbed patch of snow. 'You don't listen, lad, you don't bleedin listen!'

I didn't remember any mention of left-hander's and, even if I had, I wouldn't have known I was left-handed at rifle shooting, because I'd never done any rifle shooting.

Even if the Chief had told us about left-hander's (I was assured later that he 'bleedin well' hadn't) I, at that time, considered myself right-handed because I wrote with my right hand. Today I consider myself to be semi-ambidextrous (if, indeed, one can be): I, obviously, shoot a rifle left-handed, play snooker left-handed and I'm left-handed using a shovel, but I'm right-handed as a cricket batsman. And, although I can kick a ball effectively with my right foot, I've always relied on my left to score many a wonder goal (I wish).

I never did fully understand why lefty shooters were segregated; apparently something to do with hot, spent cartridges flying about.

We were issued with three 7.62 rounds, and managed to load them into our magazines despite having near frost bitten fingers.

'Load!' shouted the chief. Confusion: we'd already loaded our magazines. 'That means load your magazines into your bleedin rifles!' Jeez, he obviously didn't know we'd not done the mind reading course yet.

'Listen, listen. Remember, when I shout ready, cock your weapon. On commence you thumb the safety off, take aim, then pull the bleedin trigger—three times! You can remember where the bleedin trigger is, I hope!'

We all nervously glanced down.

'Target to your front, three rounds, in your own time' - that was good of him – 'COMMENCE!'

With three rounds gone and surprised by the violent kick of my weapon, I removed the magazine and made my rifle safe.

I walked to my target, hoping I'd been accurate enough and done my bit in saving the West from those pesky Eastern Bloc chaps. Oh dear: I'd only hit the target once, and that hit would have, at best, only made the ferocious soldier duck.

My neck sensed heavy breathing. 'Have you had a medical?'

'Yes, chief.'

'A full medical? Did they test your eyes?'

'They did, Chief.'

'Didn't they give you spectacles - the milk bottle bottom ones - what the Milky Bar Kid wears?'

'Err, no Chief.'

'Well they bleedin well should have!'

Now that we'd become familiar with the SLR we had to learn how to march with it. And I really enjoyed marching with my SLR, even though it was tucked neatly into my *right-hand* side. By far my favourite manoeuvre was *General Salute, Present Arms!* Over... two three... up... two three... down. Smashing! Well, it was smashing unless carrying out the manoeuvre between decks on board HMS Victory. More of that sorry episode later.

We'd also have to do our fair share of guard duty. This entailed standing to attention near the main gate and guardroom, deterring any ne'er-do-wells intent on mischief. And dressed in blue suit with white gaiters and belt, we'd take our turn with providing the marching guard during Sunday morning divisions.

Dressed for Guard Duty

Promotion!

The first week back from leave was dedicated to passing exams. We were prepared for them at school, the seamanship block, and gunnery training block.

We were threatened with being back-classed by seamanship and gunnery instructors if we failed; but the more kindly souls in school merely advised us as to what failure *might* bring.

I did well with the school exams; although just scraping through maths: a lifelong difficulty.

Seamanship went really well: I tied knots, made bends and hitches, identified different splices and ropes, and my boat work was deemed good.

Gunnery was mostly answering questions on basic trajectory: why we aimed in front of moving targets etc. The practical side was being able to load, traverse, and aim a Bofors 40/60 antiaircraft gun.

With a feeling of immense relief, on 19th January 1969 I was promoted to Junior Seaman (first class) and became a basic seaman gunner. I received the appropriate arm badges, plus five bob a fortnight added to my pay—marvellous!

Winter reluctantly relinquished its cold grip as spring took up its seasonal duty.

To prepare 41 class for a week of Work Ship, we attended a few short lessons on Ships Husbandry.

Here we learnt about all things pertaining to keeping a ship ship-shape. Because we were in the Seaman branch we concentrated mostly on the upper deck, mainly learning how to chip and scrape rust off infected paint, wire brush the infected area then repaint it, finishing with up and down brush strokes so water ran down rather than collecting on paint ridges. Made sense.

Equipped with newly acquired painting and cleaning skills we embarked on our Work Ship week. This involved keeping Ganges in ship-shape condition. Some scraped and painted buildings, some cleaned and polished inside them, whilst others brushed away winter's muck from roadways and walkways. But not me.

In 41 class was a lad we called Lucky Newsome. He was always in the right place at the right time - he'd have just left before a POI caught us having a crafty fag; be in the heads when we were turned out of our pits in the middle of the night to double round the parade ground, and many a time his kit was first out of the huge spin dryers in the laundry, so he was first outside for a crafty fag. Yes, Lucky Newsome indeed.

Well, for once, some of his luck rubbed off on me. Lucky was chosen to spend Work Ship week at the Captain's house.

Two ratings were required and I was alphabetically next on the list.

The Captain lived a short drive away in Erwarton Hall—a huge red-bricked building with lots of adjoining land. A lot of the land was set to gardens and vegetable plots. It was here that Lucky and I were set to work every morning after alighting from the back of an old rusty RN van.

My dad had an allotment growing various vegetables, but the bulk of his crop was cabbage and potatoes. My siblings and I were mainly occupied at the beginning and end of a growing season. We would do most of the digging in spring and load his hand-built wheelbarrow with cabbages in late summer, roaming the streets of Scawthorpe and Bentley, selling them for sixpence each.

Even when empty, pushing and pulling the wheelbarrow was exhausting—my dad had built it from railway sleepers, nicked from the rail line that backed onto his allotment. But we *were* rewarded with a paper cone of sugar and access to his rhubarb. Lovely!

My dad stored his potatoes in the loft at home; the abundance of his crop measured by how much the back-bedroom ceilings bowed under their weight.

So what little I knew about gardening was bolstered by knowledge imparted by the Hall gardener, especially flower growing, of which I knew nothing.

He was a grand old chap who would regale us with stories about the Hall as well as the surrounding area. According to him all the staff, past and present, and the local population, were nothing but busy-bodies. 'They mind everybody's business 'cept their own,' he would say—every day.

Lucky Newsome's luck ran out when the Captain himself caught him lounging in the kitchen, drinking tea, during our third morning. Not-so-Lucky Newsome spent the rest of Work Ship week becoming the best heads cleaner Ganges has ever known.

Working at the hall was a relief from the harshness of Ganges but, as with all good things, it came too quickly to an end.

Expedition Week

Expedition Week was our next break from the rigours of Ganges.

Normally Ganges would send juniors out into the Suffolk countryside and have them route marching, orienteering and camping. However, Ganges had volunteered a quota of its young recruits to work in a place named Wicken Fen, a nature reserve in Cambridgeshire that had been donated to the National Trust in the early 1900's.

The National Trust were expanding the reserve and making its interior more accessible by clearing and thinning out vegetation—making way for elevated wooden walk ways. We lucky lads were the ones who would be clearing the lopped trees that stood in the way of progress and profit.

We had a small village of tents to sleep in, situated behind an old, huge, three-sided barn that housed the Instructors accommodation. A corrugated iron building housed the heads, washroom, and showers.

We collected sleeping bags, which had supposedly been washed but still held a distinct sweaty odour, cooking and eating gear, and a bucket for washing it all in. Our breakfast and evening meal was cooked over an open fire—mostly sausage and beans—with bacon and eggs being provided as an occasional extravagance. A meagre packed lunch was also provided—which we shared with hordes of flying insects.

Three to a tent and Bomber, Kinky, and I had commandeered one furthest away from the barn. Well, Bomber did the commandeering; he had that 'don't argue with me' presence.

As well as the tent's location shielding us from the Instructor's prying eyes, we could empty our bladder over the nearby vegetation during the night instead of having to traipse over to the heads. Judging by the colour and sour smell of the plant life, this had been the popular option for many before us.

'How the bloody hell are we going move them trees?' moaned Kinky as we struggled into our musty sleeping bags.

'Dig em out, chop through the roots, easy bleedin peasy,' said a reassuring Bomber.

'Easy bleedin peasy! Did you not notice the size of some of em? Robin Hood could have made a home in some of em!'

'Kinky, Kinky, you're forgetting our secret weapon.'

'What's that, then?'

'Lofty.'

'No offence like,' said Kinky, looking over at me, 'but there's more meat in a NAAFI pie than there is on him.'

'Didn't stop him chopping down that skinny kid in the boxing.'

'Can't you gobby sods give it a rest,' I said, tired and peed off. 'Hey, Kinky.'

'What?'

'Blow that bloody lantern out before you get too comfy.'

'Aye aye, skipper.'

The next morning, dressed in supplied overalls and reeking wellington boots, we climbed down into the cold water of Wicken Fen. An attempt had been made to drain this part but it still held more than a foot of unpleasantly cold water - water that slopped over the top of wellies, making for uncomfortable working and possible foot rot.

As rightly guessed by the Norfolk tub of lard, we exposed the tree roots by digging round the base, where upon an experienced fens man would chop through them with a huge axe. Fear of carnage amongst the ranks forbade any junior of even thinking about wielding such a deadly weapon. And, despite Kinky's assertions, none of the trees we tackled would have tempted Robin Hood to relocate to Wicken.

Once a tree was free of its largest roots, a man driving a small crane would lift it clear of the swampy water and drag it away.

'What do you think they do with them trees, Lofty?' Kinky asked as the last tree of the day was dragged away.

'I dunno... ask Bomber, he's the tree expert.'

'Well, Bomber?'

'Log cabins.'

'Log cabins? What *are* you on about?'

'Log cabins. They build log cabins for folk to stay in, like, when this place is up and running.'

'Yeah, and me and Lofty is taking our captain exam soon as we get back to Ganges.'

'Honest...'

'Sod off, Bomber.'

A good few years ago I visited Wicken fen, and dotted around the visitors centre were some old photographs of Ganges boys working there. I didn't recognise anyone; nor were there any log cabins.

Hospitalised

Not long after our return from Wicken Fen, and returning from boat work with the inevitable doubling up and down Faith Hope and Charity, I experienced a sudden, agonising pain in my stomach.

'You, lad, you, why have you stopped?' barked Justin.

'I've got a pain, sir.' The pain increased, forcing me to double up in agony. Justin strode down to the top step of Hope.

'You'd better not be pulling a fast one, lad,' he said, poking me in the stomach with his stick. The scream I produced quelled his doubts.

'You two, Tweedy and Dooly, get this lad to the sick bay—NOW!'

Bomber and Paddy heaved me as upright as I could manage.

'What's up, then, Lofty?' asked Bomber.

'There's a right pain in my belly.'

'Makes a change from you being a pain.'

'Jeeez, not now, Bomber, not now.'

A doctor in the sick bay produced more screams, eventually diagnosing suspected appendicitis.

'Can't operate here, lad. We're more cuts and bruises now. Best get you in an ambulance to Colchester Hospital.'

Hospital? Operate? Crikey - I'd only ever seen inside a hospital watching Emergency Ward 10 on the telly. I wasn't looking forward to this—not one bit.

'We'll get your mothers contact details and send her a telegram, asking for permission to give you an anaesthetic and operate, what with you being too young and all that. Don't look so worried: it'll be over in a jiffy, and think of all those pretty nurses looking after you.'

I soon found myself on a stretcher, in an ambulance, bound for the Royal Military Hospital in Colchester. After a short time I felt something stirring in my bowls. The something caused an expulsion of wind, then another, and another, the pain in my stomach easing after each expulsion. I could see the wrinkling nose of the accompanying Sick Bay Attendant.

'Have you filled your crackers, young fella?' I answered with moans and groans, pretending to still be in agony. And I was pretending because I was scared, scared of how Ganges might punish me for making a fuss about nothing.

I knew, the same as all Ganges boys knew, that any weakness, failure, bad behaviour, or misconduct would result in some form of punishment. And I certainly wasn't looking forward to turning out of my pit at silly o'clock in the morning to clean the guardroom heads, or sweeping the Long Covered Way every Sunday afternoon. So I kept up the pretence, even when a Surgeon Commander poked and prodded my abdomen and recommended my appendix be removed as soon as my mother replied with her permission.

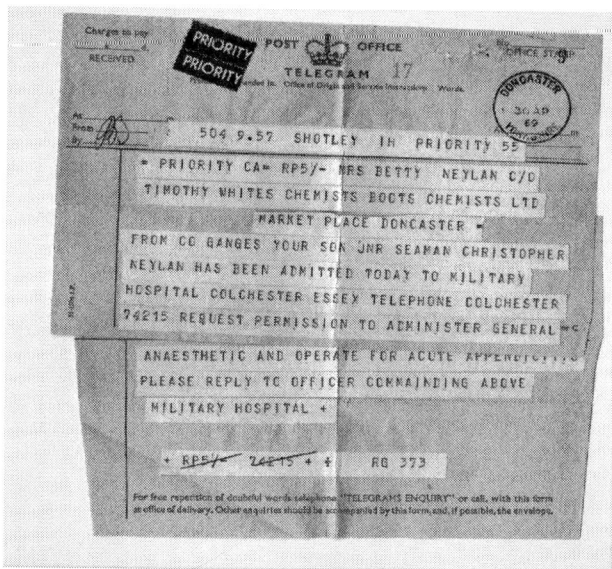

```
                                          POST      OFFICE
                         PRIORITY
                                        TELEGRAM  17
                        PRIORITY

        504 9.57  SHOTLEY  IH  PRIORITY 55

   * PRIORITY CA* RP5/- MRS BETTY  NEYLAN C/O
   TIMOTHY WHITES CHEMISTS BOOTS CHEMISTS LTD
              MARKET PLACE DONCASTER *
   FROM CO GANGES YOUR SON JNR SEAMAN CHRISTOPHER
   NEYLAN HAS BEEN ADMITTED TODAY TO MILITARY
   HOSPITAL COLCHESTER ESSEX TELEPHONE COLCHESTER
   74215 REQUEST PERMISSION TO ADMINISTER GENERAL *

   ANAESTHETIC AND OPERATE FOR ACUTE APPENDICITIS
   PLEASE REPLY TO OFFICER COMMANDING ABOVE
   MILITARY HOSPITAL +

        + RP5/-  74215 + +       RG 373
```

I awoke the next morning to find myself in a ward full of poorly men. I was dressed in hospital pyjamas which, I must say, were of a better quality than the Ganges cardboard ones. I made an attempt to pull myself up into a sitting position, but thought better of it when a sharp pain in my left side forced a wince.

'Ah, you're awake,' said an army nurse who'd suddenly appeared at the foot of my bed. 'You'll not be getting any breakfast, too soon after your op, so fill yourself up with water, drink lots of water, it'll do you good. The surgeon will be along to look you over soon. Be a good lad and don't whinge. He doesn't like whinges, the commander, he surely doesn't.'

I must have dozed off because the next thing I remember was a Surgeon Commander tapping me on the head with a clipboard.

109

'Well, well, well, the phantom appendix patient.'

Oh, no, I'd been found out.

'There was nothing at all wrong with your appendix, young man, nothing at all.'

What an idiot I'd been. Now I was in trouble.

'Still, better out than in, an appendix, better out than in,' continued the surgeon. 'Let's have a look at him, nurse. Take off his dressing, please.'

'Better out than in.' Gave me to thinking about Smiler's relationship with a lifeboat.

I couldn't believe that I'd gotten away with it. However, on reflection, I realised that it would never have occurred to the Surgeon Commander—what was he doing in a military hospital?—that anyone would fake appendicitis. Why would they? But, there again, he wasn't part of the ever and over-suspicious Ganges regime.

After a few days of recovery an army medic decided that my rate of recovery would be greatly improved if I was up and about. This was a military hospital so 'up and about' meant cleaning bedpans, sweeping the ward deck then buffering it with, thankfully, an electric device, not a boot brush, filling water jugs, and helping deliver food trays to patients at meal times. During the latter, when grumpy patients chose to find fault with their meal, I quickly learnt that it was best to say nothing rather than 'It's not my fault.'

There was a squaddie in the bed next to mine who'd suffered an unfortunate sequence of bad luck. During an operation (I forget what for) the little toe on his right foot had crossed over onto his fourth toe. Not being able to reposition the wayward digit, it had been chopped off. Unsurprisingly, he wasn't best pleased.

He was a rarity amongst strangers you meet as you travel through life. He didn't just talk about himself, like most people do, whilst boring your pants off with pictures of kids and pet animals—he was interested in who I was, my past, where I was now, and my future. No one had been that interested in my life before. It certainly boosted my self-esteem and sense of worth. Thanks, mate.

One morning, whilst in the sluice room cleaning and disinfecting bedpans, a nurse informed me that I had visitors. My first thought was that it had to be my parents, or one of them. But surely they wouldn't have the time, money or, sadly, the inclination to travel all this way—would they? No - it wasn't them.

My sister, Jane, older than me by a few years, had, by complicated association, fallen in love with a certain Les Fisher (now my brother-in-law). He was a former Ganges boy, now an Able Seaman (RP2), whose parents owned and lived in a pub, The Norfolk, in Colchester. And it was these two kind people who had come to visit me. They even brought me a box of chocolates!

Before they said their farewells, Les' parents said I was more than welcome to visit them whenever I chose, with Ganges being relatively close, and all. But Ganges shore leave didn't stretch to visiting places that far afield. However, I did go and stay with them during the rest of my Ganges long-leave holidays. Mind you, dodging the ushering instructors and ticket inspectors, and sneaking on to the London-bound train did prove somewhat difficult—even more difficult on the return journey—but it was worth it—spending my leave in a pub and not having the frustration of trying to explain Ganges—worth it indeed.

Back to reality

I'd been away for ten days, but, according to my instructors, I was doing well enough to be spared being back-classed. I was, however, placed on light duties. All this really meant was that I passed things rather than use them, and I was able to stand smugly at the side of Justin whilst the class doubled up and down Laundry Hill or Faith Hope and Charity. Nevertheless, Smiler, as only he could, found a way to abuse my new-found status.

'Light duties, lad, light duties!' I waited for Smiler's personal definition as I set about making my bed on my first evening back.

'Well, lad, make sure you're first to hear call the hands. With me so far?' He didn't wait for an answer.

'When you hear that pipe, you turn out of your pit and switch the bleedin lights on! When it's dark outside, when the ghosts and ghoulies come out to play and you hear pipe down, you switch em off! That's light duties, lad, that's light duties!' He laughed so much at his own joke I thought, and hoped, he might choke.

Later.'Hey, Lofty.'
'What...'
'Catch!'
I wasn't quick enough to catch the box of matches, and they landed on my pillow. Staring at them I think I knew what was coming next.

'You'll need them to light our first fag in the morning. That's light duties, lad, that's light duties!'
'Sod off, Bomber!'
Kinky was beside himself: 'Nice one, Bomber, nice one!'

Sea Experience

HMS Ulster was originally a U class destroyer, commissioned for service during the Second World War. In 1956 she was converted to a Type 15 Frigate. When I got to know her in 1969 she was attached to HMS Dryad (where the 'no thickness detected' Radar Plotters trained) for training and trials of newly developed navigation equipment.

Sitting in the NAAFI canteen one Saturday afternoon in May, swigging from bottles of Dandelion and Burdock, relaxing after Saturday rounds and a fraught kit muster, the topic of conversation was dominated by Class 41's impending Sea Experience.

'The Ulster, in Portsmouth,' said Kinky. 'Never been to Portsmouth.'

'Is that in Ireland?' asked Reedy.

'Portsmouth, in Ireland? Are you bleedin thick, or what?' snapped Kinky.

'No, Ulster, gob shite.'

'Is it Paddy?'

'Yeah, I'm an Ulster boy, so I am.'

'Well, with a ship full of Ulster men you'll feel right at home like,' said Kinky.

We all agreed that Kinky talked shite, most of the time, and were surprised that Paddy hadn't thumped him.

Because there just wasn't room for twenty or so would-be sailors to be accommodated on board the Ulster, we messed in a large hut in HMS Dryad.

In Dryad's galley, at breakfast and supper time, it was fascinating to see saucer-eyed RP trainees manoeuvring cutlery on tables, then hear them shouting 'course to intercept, course to intercept!' I think, on the whole, the dessert spoons won.

'Now, you lot,' said Justin, as we gathered at the bottom of Ulster's gangway, staring up at this (to us) huge ship with the gleaming red hand of Ulster painted onto its funnel. 'When we're aboard, if anyone tells you to do something, you do it, and smartly! Understood?'

'Yes, SIR!'

'And!'

'Understood, SIR!'

'And do not forget to salute the quarter deck. Follow me, then. Single file, single file.'

Up the gangway we went, saluting to our right as we reached the brow, and then followed Justin to muster on the quarter deck, where we were met by a stout, grey-bearded chief petty officer.

'Ah, Ganges lads, always welcome, Ganges lads. I was a Ganges lad.' He paused, looking lost in good or bad memories. 'Are they good lads, Petty Officer Case?'

'Mostly, but I think they're too used to bricks and concrete, bo's'n. Do em good to find some sea legs and see what all the training's for.' (Bo's'n, pronounced Bosun—master and fierce custodian of the upper deck.)

'Well, we'll get em below and they'll see how lucky they are to be messing in the vast spaces of a stone frigate.' (Shore establishment.)

'Follow me down, lads, follow me down'—would I eventually talk like a parrot—'face your front, don't turn round or we'll be here 'till evening rounds!'

At some speed the bo's'n disappeared down the hatch. We followed at a more sedate pace—our idea of descending ladders turned on its head.

'This,' said the bo's'n, after we'd managed the unnatural ladder descent, 'is the main passageway. Some old hands still call it the Burma Road. Think of it as the same as your Long Covered Way—everywhere important leads off it. Gunners usually mess forrard—follow me!'

We walked forrard, passing ladders and hatches, the bo's'n explaining where they lead to, and walking through unclipped, watertight doors. There was always the deep, throbbing sound of machinery working somewhere, and a pervasive smell that seemed to consist mostly of fuel oil and stewed cabbage.

The forward seaman's mess was a huge shock: how could twelve men live in these cramped conditions? There wasn't room to swing an Instructors stick, let alone a cat-o'-nine tails.

'Looks a lot better now, since we became a Frigate,' the bo's'n said. 'See, some gunners have the luxury of bunks. The others stow their hammocks over there, in the hammock netting. On your first ship, being juniors, you'll be getting a hammock to sleep in if it's a bunk and hammock mess.'

'Did you have a hammock on your first ship, sir?' asked Chalky.

'I'm a chief, son, not a sir, but, yes, a hammock was all we had.'

'When did you join your first ship, sir, sorry, chief?' persisted Chalky.

'Young fella, when I joined my first ship the Dead Sea was just unwell.' Justin laughed, but we didn't get it.

'Lots more to see. Up this ladder to the upper deck and fo'c'sle, then we'll make our way aft. Tomorrow, tomorrow we'll be putting to sea, so it's best you know where your lifeboat station is, in case we have to abandon ship. Don't look so worried, I've never had to abandon ship—yet.' The bo's'n chuckled as he led the way up the ladder.

The next morning saw us once again mustered on the quarterdeck. It felt strange, standing still on a quarterdeck. I think we all had an instinctive urge to come to attention and double on the spot. But we weren't there for long before the bo's'n took us forrard to muster between the bridge ladders on the fo'c'sle.

'Watch and learn, lads, watch and learn,' advised the bo's'n as the call came for hands to muster on deck for leaving harbour.

'Special sea dutymen to your stations; assume damage control state one, condition Zulu Alpha,' came a calm but authoritative voice through the tannoy system. 'Single up, fore and aft!'

We watched as the fo'c'sle hands, responding to 'let go' orders, heaved in the remaining ropes until all that was left holding Ulster alongside was a wire rope.

'See that wire rope,' said Justin, pointing to a rope whose eye was over a jetty bollard, just in front of Ulsters bow, the other end belayed around a fo'c'sle bollard.

'That's the head spring. With a little tickle of the starboard engine ahead, that will tighten and the stern will swing out. See the two men with fenders lowered? That'll stop any nasty scrapes to the bow if it swings in too much. When the stern is out and away, we'll let go the spring and go astern both (engines). We'll then straighten up and go ahead, out of the harbour and into the Solent —as easy as that!'

The Ulster manoeuvred just as Justin predicted, and we were soon out in the Solent with Southsea Castle on our port beam. We'd helped (often hindered) the fo'c'sle men to stow hawsers and wire rope, and been rewarded with a mug of hot, sweet stand-easy tea, and a sticky bun.

The weather was good as Ulster cut through a light swell, with only a fine spray coming over her bows. It felt grand to be at sea, standing on the deck of a warship that belonged to the greatest navy in the world.

Some didn't feel so grand. Some looked to be in various stages of queasiness.

'You're looking a bit pasty, Kinky,' said Bomber.

'Must have been something I had for breakfast.'

'Yeah, right. You, Reedy, Alfie, and Lucky must have had the same.'

Justin interrupted: 'If any of you are going to heave up, do it over the lee side, the side with the wind at your back.' Made sense.

Ulster was well into the Solent when we visited the ops room. Crammed into the small space we listened as a petty officer, with zig zaggy lines on his arm badge, explained what was happening.

'We're testing some new navigational equipment today,' he said. It was good that we were all crammed together because only bats would have heard him if we were on deck—he was very quietly spoken.

He continued: 'Without the Navigation officer and his Yeoman having to consult their charts, we're relying on this new equipment,' he pointed to a brightly lit oval screen, manned by a bloke in a white smock, 'to take us around the Isle of Wight. I can't tell you anymore because it's top secret. If you do tell anyone you've been in here and what you've seen—and I mean anyone—even your parents in a letter, then you'll be found out, court marshalled and hanged for treason at HMS Drake.' The ops room ratings sniggered, even the boffin in the white smock sniggered.

Justin fuelled the micky taking: 'And if it fails, PO?'

'Well, we'll either end up lost in the middle of the English Channel, or get battered to bits on a rocky coastline.'

Someone made a dash for the ops room door.

'Lee side, Dewer, lee side!'

As junior ratings, no matter which ship we first served in, having the micky taken was part and parcel of being inducted into life in the RN.

Ulster successfully circumnavigated the Isle of Wight, and as she re-entered harbour and came alongside her berth—we watched and learnt, watched and learnt.

We didn't put to sea again, which rather made a mockery of Sea Training. But the bo's'n did school us in all aspects of seamanship—from anchors and cables to tying, splicing, and whipping rope.

Justin schooled us in the ship's layout, how to assume different damage control states and, most importantly, ship etiquette.

'When you join your first ship,' Justin told us, 'you'll be the lowest of the low—unless there are midshipmen aboard—and the way you conduct yourself and speak to crew will determine your quality of life. In other words—don't be a lazy, scruffy gob shite!'

Why did most of us shoot a glance towards Kinky?

Blowin' in the Wind

When I was no' but a lad, we made trolleys out of planks of wood and old pram wheels. Old prams could, curiously, be found abandoned in ditches almost anywhere.

On Saturday mornings, every few months or so, we could get free entry into the Collar (Coliseum) picture house in Bentley, just by producing an empty PG Tips box.

There we would watch cowboys fight with pesky Indians, Germans losing the war and, my favourite, pirates pinching chests of gold from law-abiding seafarers and each other.

But it wasn't the deck skirmishes, or broadsides sending cannon shot tearing through masts and rigging that most thrilled me; it was pirate ships making sail then making haste to board the next victim.

The trolleys we made were heavy and had to be pushed a fair way to the top of the hill on Pipering Lane.

One year, when the autumn winds arrived, my elder brother, Andy, and I, inspired by pirate films, had a go at harnessing the wind to ease the burden of trolley pushing. I was keen to have a go because Andy, being the eldest, mostly steered whilst I did most of the pushing.

So, with an old clothes prop, six inch nails pilfered from my dad's stash, and an old sheet, we attempted to harness the wind. We had little success because, obviously, we were reliant on the wind blowing in the direction we wanted to go.

And that, mostly, is why I became hooked when Justin introduced us to the Boson's Dinghy as part of our boat work training. Justin taught us the basics then, because dinghy sailing was his passion, gave extra tuition to those who were interested. If only my brother and I knew then what Justin later taught me.

The annual Divisional sailing regatta was held during the week before Ganges summer leave. Competing in the dingy class with me was my sailing partner Ian Rose. We'd practised a lot during our free time, and were confidant of giving a good account of ourselves—maybe even winning our event. I'd told him about my trolley days, but he just thought I was off mine.

Between two buoys at the imaginary start line we were one of six dinghies, with sails luffing, ready for the off.

The claxton sounded, sheets were tightened, and we all headed down river for the red buoy, that we would round and sail back to the start line, that would, in turn, become the finishing line.

We made good headway, tacking into a head wind. I was on the sail sheets, leaving Rosy on the boom and tiller (I'd lost the toss). Instead of time-consuming going about at the buoy, our cunning plan was to gybe around it and allow the following wind to blow us to victory.

We thought it a good plan until a sudden wind shift occurred just as the boom went over and I'd loosed the sheets. Instead of following the boom with the tiller, a panicking Rosy pushed it over the other way, and the dingy, not knowing what was expected of her, decided enough was enough—and capsized.

We'd practised capsizing and righting as part of our training, but nothing could have prepared us for keeling over in the middle of a freezing estuary. Thank goodness for the warmth of a summer day.

We quickly righted the dingy and managed to tip and empty most of the seawater. We found some comfort, but very little, when we saw another dingy being righted just aft of us.

'Come on, Lofty, if we're quick, at least we won't be last.'

'Last, chuffin last! You're worried about being last! Justin's going to have us scrub out every dingy, whaler, cutter, and canoe before we go on leave.'

'Canoes?'

'Well, maybe not canoes...'

'Aw, come on, we got into trouble and got out of it. Justin will be proud of us.'

'We, chuffin we?'

'You'd best take the tiller, Lofty. It's not been my best tiller day.'

'Have you ever had a good one? Starboard tack, then, keep those bloody sheets tight... and every time I look you'd better be bailing.'

All hopes of salvaging any modicum of dignity were dashed as the other distressed dinghy overhauled us and beat its way to the finishing line.

Sod it!

Justin didn't seem too bothered when he caught up with us, after we'd showered and changed. Maybe his thoughts were with enjoying his approaching leave. Who knows, but we were thankful, very thankful.

'Whose idea was it to gybe?' he asked.

We confessed to it being a joint decision.

'So you don't remember me telling you that only accomplished, that means *real sailors,* attempt to gybe in an estuary?'

'Yes, sir, sorry sir, but we thought it a good idea and worth a try,' replied Rosy. I let Rosy do all the replying, just hoping he'd stop digging a hole we couldn't get out of.

Justin thought for a moment then gave his opinion: 'Well, on the scale of good ideas, I'd rate it somewhere between volunteering for submarines and invading Russia in winter. But it was worth a try: trying *is* the Ganges way, after all.'

121

Crikey, Justin was in a good mood. He must be going somewhere really special for his leave, or looking forward to sending his latest batch of nozzers into the wide Navy world.

and Beyond...

HMS Cambridge

Wednesday October 1st 1969

The few weeks after summer leave were filled with, well, nothing really. Ganges had done its best for us and was ready to send its latest batch of newly trained Junior Seaman to their next, designated training establishment. For Gunnery ratings this meant HMS Cambridge, a gunnery school located on windswept Wembury Point, near Plymouth.

Justin accompanied his class to see them safely board the overnight train to Plymouth. He wished us luck as we boarded, and bid us farewell.

All in all, Justin was a decent and fair bloke, and had done his best to prepare 41 class for life in the wider reaches of the Royal Navy. I hope he's living a happy life.

There are some things, good or bad, that you can't leave in the past. Some things, like Ganges, follow you all through your life. Ganges, for me, was a good thing.

The RN ramshackle of a coach drove through HMS Cambridge's main gate, followed by a lorry that held our kit. We were driven up a steep incline towards the main establishment and accommodation. Here, the messes weren't arranged like those at Ganges: they were stacked on top of each other in brick-built blocks, and looked to be fairly new builds.

A POGI (Petty Officer Gunnery Instructor) met us as we struggled to retrieve our kit from the lorry.

'Morning, lads. Good journey?' As usual there was no wait for an answer. 'I'm PO Winter and some of you will be under my wing for the short time you're here. You'll be messing in Anson block, six to a room'—room? 'So get in there, sort your kit and yourselves out, shower and change into No. 8's and I'll be back just before dinner. Any questions?'

'No, SIR!'

'I'm not a sir, PO will do, and there is no need to shout. Well... look lively!'

Bomber, as was his way, barged to the front leading me, Kinky, Rosy, Alfie, and Paddy Dooley up a flight of stairs and into the first empty mess we came to. It was then we understood 'room'. It was a room, a room with only three beds arranged on either side. And each bed came with a wardrobe! Not a large wardrobe, but much larger than the Ganges lockers; and you were allowed to close the doors.

We could hang things up—WOW! And it had an enclosed shelf at the top and two draws at the bottom. This wardrobe arrangement meant that we couldn't possibly stow our kit with our names displayed the Ganges way, although Kinky did try— bless him.

We were gobsmacked, to say the least. This was a sudden and, in many respects, an unsettling new way of life and we were lost in it. But help was at hand: there was a notice board behind the door with a routine and list of do's and don'ts.

'Well things haven't changed that much,' said Alfie, reading from the notice board. 'There's evening rounds and, hey... look at this.'

'Look at what?'

'It sez that every duty watchman will be responsible for reporting for duty at his given station ten minutes before his watch starts.'

We'd been taught the Navy's watch system but thought we'd be doing those at sea on our first ship. But there was a caveat.

'Ah, this is better,' continued Alfie, 'junior ratings will only be required to stand the last-dog and first watches.'

'I wouldn't worry too much about all that,' said Kinky, finally abandoning his name alignment and bestowing POGI Winter with a nickname, 'Chilly will fill us in on what's what.' And he did.

About an hour before dinner, Chilly rounded up 41 class and led us into a classroom in the teaching block. There he announced the demise of 41 class by splitting us into two new classes: JG25 and JG26. I, along with some of my closest 41 class mates, including Bomber, were in JG26—Chilly's class.

Chilly presented us with when, where, and what timetables and a duty watch rota. Then tried to explain them to his new, bemused class.

'Where' consisted of a grand tour of Cambridge. The flat land atop the point, as well as the accommodation blocks, held a NAAFI canteen, bar (not for us), shop and a laundrette. The laundrette was something of a wonderment. It was permanently open, so queuing wasn't much of a problem.

Except for the huge contraption in Ganges, I don't think any of us had ever seen an automatic washing machine. We were used to twin tubs and, in Bomber's case, wash tub and mangle. There was even a drying machine. Marvellous!

Down a short incline, towards the sea, concrete terraces had been built into the cliffs. The top terrace housed gun direction platforms, radar masts, and all kinds of technical-looking devices that ensured a fired shell or missile achieved its maximum, destructive capability.

The terrace below held an array of weapons, from Oerlikon 20mm cannons to 4. 5 inch gun turrets, with accompanying 'ready-use' shell magazines. There were a few shrouded missile launches, but we didn't get to see underneath the shrouds during our short training time.

The bottom terrace housed various buildings that contained offices and more technical wizardry.

'Most of your time,' said Chilly, 'will be spent loading, unloading, laying, and training—aiming to you—and cleaning guns.'

'Shells are an expensive item and you'll probably not get to do any live firing. These days it's mostly boffins checking and improving firing systems. Anyway, you'll soon be blasting away on your first ship and dripping'—moaning—'like a wet awning when you're sponging out and securing in roughers— rough sea, that's a rough sea.' He'd noticed our puzzled looks.

The next morning found us assembled at the side of a pedestal-mounted 20mm Oerlikon twin-barrelled cannon. We spent the morning changing barrels, removing and replacing the sixty-round drum magazines and setting the sights. Needless to say I spent most of the morning on tiptoes.

After dinner, tuition was more technically based: viable targets, rate of fire, and trajectory. All of which had to be remembered if we wanted to pass our final gunnery exam.

And so the days passed with us moving on to the Bofors 40/60 (apparently the size of the shell could be fitted into the length of the barrel 60 times, or was somebody having us on?) and the Mark 6, 4.5inch twin turret. We could all manage the brass cartridge when loading, but a fifty-two pound 4.5inch shell was a very different matter for some of us.

Life was busy and training demanding, with constant monitoring of our ability. But we still felt lost in this different regime: even evening rounds was just a peek through the door by the duty officer. He didn't inspect us, or our kit, and then send us doubling up and down the terraces as punishment for any found faults. And I'm sure we'd have all welcomed Chilly thrashing the end of our bed every morning and overseeing the deck being polished every evening. Well, maybe not *every* morning and not *every* evening.

Normal just wasn't normal anymore.

And festering at the back of our minds was the certainty of having to adapt, yet again, when we joined our first sea-going ship in just a few short weeks. Those weeks were extended for two of our classmates who were deemed not to be making expected progress.

Our watch keeping duties weren't too demanding. Leaving the guardroom, armed with a torch, all we had to do was take turns roaming the terraces, seeking out spies and terrorists, and swapping different coloured metal tallies, which were housed in little boxes, to deter any dereliction of duty. But it was spooky, especially on your own when autumn storms were

127

rampant. It sounds funny now, but a cruel trick was played on Alfie one stormy night.

The most isolated tally box lay at the very eastern end of the Point. Someone, or two, had managed to catch a cat and then managed to stuff it into the box and wedge the door shut. According to the two most senior ranked watch keepers sent to find absent Alfie, he was huddled beside a low wall blubbering, and as white as a sheet in a DAZ advert.

Shore leave was restricted by the lack of local buses and the special 22:00 return bus from Plymouth to Cambridge. After 21:00 we would be absent without leave, so we spent most of our free time in the canteen. But, quite often, especially at weekends, we would walk a cliff path to a pub in Heybrook Bay and take advantage of the Landlord's 'blind eye'. But he would only turn his blind eye if we hid behind the large jukebox to sup our illicitly bought bottles of Double Diamond.

Sea Survival Training

Conversely, or so we ignorantly thought, the RAF would be responsible for our sea survival training.

On a cold morning, near the end of October, with a spare set of No. 8s and sea jersey, the eight remaining members of CJ26 class boarded the back of a rickety RN lorry for the short journey to RAF Mount Batten, which was situated up the coast near Plymouth Sound.

Once there, in a nautically adorned room, a stern looking RAF officer gave detailed tuition on the many aspects of sea survival, then outlined the particular training course we would be undertaking. We were then, literally, dumped into the practical side.

An RAF fast rescue boat took us out into a choppy Plymouth sound, hove to and threw an inflatable liferaft over the side. Those under training, thankfully wearing life jackets, soon followed.

The shock of the cold water was quickly overridden by the instinct for survival as we made for the life raft. Swimming on your back and not doggy paddling had been the given advice, but some were too panicked to heed it, so boat hooks were used to prod any wayward swimmers towards relative safety.

The job of the first survivor of the hypothetical sinking ship we'd jumped off to reach the liferaft was to pull the inflation handle. I was immensely relieved to see a bright-orange bag swell into an essential bit of life saving kit. Someone had had a remarkably good swim—it definitely wasn't Bomber.

Once we were all in the raft and in the early throes of survival, the FRB stood off, keeping a watchful eye as we attempted to complete various tasks.

After rigging devices to collect fresh water, and attempting to unravel the mysteries of some navigational equipment—all the time hampered by bouts of vomiting, shivering, and the ever itching sea jerseys—our last task was to fire off flares that would, hopefully, reveal our position to a searching helicopter.

We heard the whirling rotor blades just seconds before an enormous pair of boots came crashing through the raft's canopy doorway. The winchman dragged the survivor he'd landed on into a harness, then they both disappeared skyward.

My turn.

I don't remember too much detail because my eyes shut tight as soon as the harness tightened, and I only opened them when my feet touched down on the deck of the FRB. I do not like heights!

Showered, changed and carrying my clean sea jersey—the itching was worse than being cold—and warmed on the inside by a welcome bowl of hot soup, I joined CJ26 class to board the rickety truck for the return to Cambridge.

ROYAL AIR FORCE

SEA SURVIVAL TRAINING

This is to certify that

P109185   J S C. NEYLAN

has satisfactorily completed a course of training in Sea Survival and has with fortitude undergone the rigorous requirements of this School

DATE 28th October 1969

Flight Lieutenant
For Officer Commanding
School of Combat Survival and Rescue,
Royal Air Force, Mount Batten.

Pier Head Jump

Five weeks of training culminated with the obligatory final exams. On the Sunday evening before they started, JG26 class were huddled around a table in the NAFFI canteen.

'What kind of questions do you think there'll be?' asked Alfie to no one in particular.

'Why, you worried?' replied Rosy, sounding uncharacteristically concerned.

'Bomber hopes they'll all be about muck spreading,' chimed in Kinky.

'And I'll be spreading you all over this canteen, gob shite. Are you really worried, Alfie, about passing?'

'Yeah, don't want to be back classed.'

'So you're worried about your future, like.'

'Yeah, it gets shorter with every bloody exam I have to take.'

'Sit next to Lofty and copy, then... he's a bit of a swot... but don't copy his name... that might give the game away... especially as he don't know how to spell it.'

'So...'

'Yeah. Lofty, I know... sod off!'

Early on Monday morning, as I sat at my little desk, trying to write the correct drill for dealing with a 4.5inch gun miss-fire—angling my paper as much as I dare towards Alfie—my Divisional Officer walked into the room.

'Sorry, chief,' he said to the presiding CGI, 'have you a Junior Seaman Neylan here?' The CGI looked down at a piece of paper.

'Yes, sir. Would you like a word?'

'Yes, please.'

Well I must have done something wrong, even if I couldn't remember what it was, I thought, as I followed my DO. My last image of the room was Bomber drawing an index finger across his throat. It didn't help.

And so began my 'Pier Head Jump' (a sudden, mostly unwelcome draft to another ship).

'Don't look so worried,' said my DO as he invited me to take a seat in his small office. 'How would you like to go to Malta?' Malta? I'd heard of Malta, but hadn't the foggiest where it was.

'The Torquay have a rating short, the ship's butcher, to be exact. You'll be flying out to replace him.' Butcher? Me? 'Go and pack your kit, all of it. You have about half an hour before transport takes you to Plymouth station. From there you'll travel to Swindon and the RAF will pick you up from there.'

'But, sir, I didn't finish my exam paper.'

'Don't worry about that: you've passed, with flying colours.' Now where had I heard that before?

'Off you go, then, lad. Make sure you're packed and ready in half an hour and dressed in your No. 2s. Here's your travel warrant. Oh, we'll let your parents know where you've gone.

But just in case we forget, send them a postcard. Good luck, off you go, off you go.'

At about 1pm I was being driven to RAF Brize Norton in an RAF staff car, no less. It was a comfortable ride but I was far from comfortable with the quick change in my circumstances: I hadn't had time to get my head around flying to join my first sea-going ship, and as a butcher—a butcher! But worse, much worse, I hadn't even had the chance to say goodbye to Bomber. I don't know why, probably the nature of serving in the Royal Navy—new ships, new mates—but I never did see or hear from Bomber again, or any of my other Ganges mates. I hope, like Justin, they are all living a happy life.

After what seemed like no time at all I found myself standing beside a huge Britannia cargo plane. After checking my newly acquired RN ID card, a member of the plane's crew helped me with my kit as I boarded. He stowed it in some kind of bag netting that hung from the bulkhead of the plane's huge, empty hold.

'Stay there, I'll be back,' said the crewman. He disappeared, then reappeared carrying a metal-framed seat. He bolted it to the floor then told me to sit on it.

'A last-minute passenger—and the only one. You must be important. I'll be back with some food and a drink once we've been airborne for a while.'

He paused as he strapped me into my seat. 'Be in Malta in about four hours, give or take. Don't let the noise frighten you...it's normal... press that buzzer if you need the toilet.'

The noise was the least of my concerns: here I was, being delivered into the unknown and unfamiliar—again.

A RN van was waiting for my arrival at RAF Luqa. The driver was a Maltese civilian who must have been surprised by the wraith-like figure, standing with his kit, looking lost and forlorn.

'HMS Torquay?'

'Yeah, that's me.'

'Fine ship, fine ship. You been Malta before?'

'No,' I replied, feeling uncomfortably warm in my blue-serge uniform.

'Ha, I thought not: you a very young boy, too young and too small to be this far from home.'

I replied with all the manliness I could muster—'I'm sixteen.'

'No matter, I will look after you. We will go the long way and let you see some of my beautiful island.'

Malta is a beautiful little island and I really appreciated the driver's kindness in showing me some of its many delights. However, it was something of a culture shock: I was used to rows of brick-built terraced houses, their fronts guarded by privet hedges, and backyards turned to lawn or seasonal vegetable plots. There wasn't much greenery in Malta and the buildings were mostly timber and sandstone built.

Yes, a different world, but I had a sense of superiority over those I'd left behind in Doncaster. Most of those people would never get the chance to share my cultural experiences. My chosen career didn't seem to be such a bad choice after all.

HMS Torquay

HMS Torquay was one of six Type 12 Whitby Class frigates (commonly known as the Seaside Class) laid down and built in the middle 50's, with various modifications added over the years until being de-commissioned and scrapped in the 80's. The other ships were the Tenby, Scarborough, Eastbourne, Blackpool and the Whitby herself. All had a complement of about 200.

The prominent feature of the class was the long and wider Vee Form Bow, which made it possible and more comfortable for the crew, for the ship to be driven into heavy seas without troughing (cresting waves and crashing into the trough between) and directing spray away from the fo'c'sle.

Ideal for the Class's initial primary role as convoy escorts in the North Atlantic. Obviously never needed for that role, they were deployed as anti-submarine frigates throughout NATO friendly waters. Apart from, that is, the Whitby, which had the nickname 'Wandering Whitby' because she wandered, by herself, more or less, all over the world.

Armament consisted of one 4.5inch twin turret, two single-barrel 40/60 Bofors and two aft mounted triple-barrelled A/S mortars.

HMS Torquay

⚓

The Torquay's quartermaster, observing my arrival, sent down his mate to assist me with my kit—very thoughtful—and before long I was down below in the coxswain's little office. The coxswain (pronounced cox's'n; shortened to 'swain, by those allowed to do so), is a small ships sheriff and senior helmsman when a ship is entering or leaving harbour.

'Sit down, lad, sit down,' said the cox's'n, a small, wiry man of Scottish decent. 'You're our new butcher,' he noticed the questioning look on my face. 'Don't worry, you'll not be carving up any animals; those days are long gone. The thing is, we only have a few cooks and their time is spent feeding the crew at all hours. All you have to do is bring up bits and pieces from the freezer for them, as and when. Butcher is just a title from the past—better than being called the cooks skivvy.'

'You'll also be responsible for cleaning the galley flat and slicing the frozen bread every morning—don't worry, you'll not be using your rigging knife... we have a bread slicer. The good news, for you at any rate, is you'll only be the butcher until we arrive back in Devonport. I should be getting a replacement for you there. You need to be learning all the things a junior seaman gunner needs to learn—the sooner the better. You don't say much, do you?'

I was trying to make sense of what he was saying: freezer, galley flat, frozen bread... frozen bread?

'Sorry, sir, I was...'

'Still stuck in the Ganges regime? You only address officers as sir. All ratings above able seaman you address them according to rank. Yes?'

'Yes, err...'

'cox's'n.'

'Yes, cox's'n.'

'You'll soon get used to it. You won't be doing any watches, but you will be spending time in the wheelhouse and the chief gunner will be teaching you all things gunnery. Your special sea duty station is the fo'c'sle. Yes?'

'Yes, cox's'n.' I agreed without a clue as to what I was agreeing to

'You'll be in the forrard seaman's mess. The mess Killick will meet you there. I'll get somebody to help you with your kit. Oh, and your pay will be in the currency of where we are or where we're going—not always pounds and pennies.'

'Mine goes into the Post Office, cox's'n.'

'You're in the grown-up Navy now, young un. Put the money you've saved, if you've saved any, where you want to when we get back to Devonport.'

I was met in my new home by the Leading Seaman (Killick) of the mess: Leading Seaman Duncan.

'What's your name, young un?'

'Junior Seaman Neylan.'

'That much I know; what's your first name?'

137

'Christopher, Chris, Leading Seaman Duncan.'

'Ha-ha,' he laughed. 'Your nozzer days are over, young un. Down here you can call me George. Anywhere else it's Hookey,' he pointed to the anchor badge on his shirt sleeve. 'Did you have a Ganges nickname? Most lads did.'

'Yes, Hookey, sorry George. It was lofty.'

'I can understand that. So, lofty it is. Oh, one other thing: you'll be with me on the fo'c'sle. Stick close to me and listen and learn. Oh, there is something else: down here you only speak when you're spoken to, until you've settled in, and don't be down here when we're having our tot. You're not one of those cocky, cheeky sods, are you?' He didn't wait for an answer—so much for my 'nozzer days' being over. 'Let's get your kit stowed and I'll show you where you'll be slinging your hammock.'

My locker was even smaller than the one at Ganges, but George introduced me to all manner of kit-stowing secrets, and all the nooks and crannies where surplus kit could be stowed.

I quickly got used to life in a mess in a real ship. I was the only junior seaman down there and my experienced messmates quickly took me under their wing—helping me sling my hammock, meal routines, washing, dhobiing, and all other things mess and ship related.

Occasionally they took me ashore with them, introducing me to the vicarious area known as 'the Gut'. But I was always sent back onboard to meet my curfew time of 21:00.

We sailed (corrective pedantics said 'steamed'- we didn't have sails) for home at the end of November, calling in at Gibraltar to refuel, where a sad yet amusing incident took place.

Down in the forrard seaman's mess was an able seaman who everybody called 'Black Pig'. All I can remember of him is that he was a scruffy individual who kept himself to himself, and the only time I saw him was when he was laying, smelling, in his bottom bunk. George, surprisingly, for some reason, chose to ignore his existence. Looking back now I think the poor bloke must have had some mental health issues—George must have had similar thoughts.

Walking back to the dockyard after a few brief hours buying 'goodies' for the folks back home, three of us came across Black Pig sprawled in the gutter outside a pub. No matter our opinion of Black Pig, he was a member of our ship, our mess, and with him not looking too well we decided to help him up and stagger to the nearby hospital—everywhere on Gibraltar is nearby.

We were met by a nurse as we helped him stagger down a long corridor.

'He doesn't look too well,' she said, 'has he been drinking?'

'Can't have had that much,' replied Taffy Turner, 'can't have been ashore for long.'

'Okay, follow me,' we followed her further down the corridor and into, what looked to be, an examination room.

'Sit him on that bed and I'll have a look.'

She gave Black Pig a brief examination, not getting any response to any of the questions she asked.

'No, I don't think it's all down to drink. I'll get a doctor to have a look at him. What's his name?' We gave her a puzzled look.

'Err... Black Pig,' was the only name Tug Wilson could come up with.

'Is he a pirate?' Her tone of voice suggested she was being nothing but serious.

We left the hospital laughing quietly and wondering if anyone would believe our—'is he a pirate'—Black Pig story.

We sailed from Gibraltar, without Black Pig, and arrived back in Guzz (Navy name for Plymouth) in time for Christmas leave.

Nothing much had changed at home and it was, again, frustrating trying to explain life in the Royal Navy, especially the question: 'what's your cabin like?' Yes, very frustrating.

1970 loomed large with the beginning, in earnest, of my seamanship and gunnery training. I was fortunate that HMS Torquay was part of the Dartmouth Training Squadron, formed to train aspiring midshipmen. Fortunate on two accounts.

First, most of the senior and leading ratings were specialists in their fields; therefore I was trained by the best. Secondly there were midshipmen (middies) aboard, so I was no longer the lowest of the low.

We formed a small DTS squadron, sailing with the Tenby and Eastbourne.

Early into 1970 our small Flotilla left Devonport for a 'Good Will' and 'Flag Waving' tour, visiting home ports and other NATO countries.

For the home part the three ships went their separate ways—reforming before we sailed over the North Sea to Kiel.

Torquay was our first destination. Being situated just around the corner it didn't take long to get there. It seemed that all the local people had turned out to greet us as we entered its small harbour.

The Mayor and his wife came aboard and, because I was the youngest rating, I was given the honour of presenting the Mayor's wife with a bouquet of flowers, tied in the middle with a Torquay cap tally. It might well have been an honour, but I had to dress in my No.1 suit—I'd spent the previous evening finding it then ironing it!

There were also groups of school kids being shown around the upper deck; their excitement curbed by the certain knowledge that they'd have to write about it upon their return to school.

Our next visit was to the Pool of London (where HMS Belfast was permanently moored just over a year later).

'Coming ashore with us, Lofty? See the bright lights,' asked George.

'Yeah, thanks, never been here before.'

'It's a very busy place, full of tourists and the like,' said Willy Williams, 'don't be tempted by the ladies and lose us.'

'I won't.'

But I did.

We went ashore in the early evening, intent on seeing some of the capital's sights; but the things to see soon turned to seeing inside the pubs we came across.

After a few hours of 'pub seeing'—George making sure I only drank pop—I was slow catching up with my messmates as they ventured further into the heart of London. I thought I'd seen them turn left at a junction, so I confidently followed.

But they were nowhere to be seen, so it didn't take me long to realise I'd lost them so, subsequently, I was lost. I well knew my geographical limitations - I could get lost in a beach hut. No bother, I'd get a fast black (taxi).

Time and time again I stuck my arm out, trying to wave down a taxi (I'd seen how it was done on the telly), but none stopped. Maybe they saw sailors as bad customers or even bad omens. I didn't know; but what I did know was that time was passing quickly and I was in danger of being adrift (late onboard).

Eventually, after following directions from some kind London folk, I made it back to the Torquay—alas, thirty minutes adrift.

As I clambered onboard I was hoping to see a friendly quartermaster who might, just might, hand me back my watch card with a warning. Well, he might have done if the Officer of the watch hadn't been standing beside him.

'21:30,' the officer said, looking at his watch, 'that makes you, what, thirty minutes adrift?'

'Yes, sir, sorry sir.'

'Do you have an excuse; one I haven't heard before?'

'I couldn't flag down a taxi, sir, so I had to walk. I was lost, you see...'

'Well I haven't heard that one before, but it's as unbelievable as most I've heard.' He let out a disbelieving sigh. 'London and you couldn't get a taxi? Unbelievable, ruddy unbelievable.'

'But it is true, sir, none of them would stop.'

'Well, good luck with that story when you're in front of the First Lieutenant's defaulters table in the morning. 0900 hours—DO NOT BE LATE!'

The Jimmy (First Lieutenant, second in command on a small ship) didn't believe my story either, so handed me two days stoppage of pay and leave. And it was some time before people stopped shouting 'Taxi!' as I went about my duties.

The next morning we slipped our moorings and made our way back down the Thames—but not without incident.

After a ship left its moorings in front of an audience, it was naval custom for its upper deck crew to line the ship. If the audience were important enough, we would wear our No. 2s. Very important, No.1's. There couldn't have been any dignitaries watching our departure, so we wore No. 2s.

After clearing the main area of the capital, and then being dismissed from ship-lining, I made my way below. I chose to go down a midship hatch, hoping to scrounge a mug of tea from the galley before I went to change.

The hatch I went down was immediately above one of the engine room hatches. As I descended I was met by a rising ball

143

of flame that seared the insides of my bell-bottom trousers. I scrambled back up and fell backward over the hatching. A firm, meaty hand gripped my collar.

'If you want to jump ship, young un, best over the guard rail than under it,' said a PO as he hauled me to my feet.

'There's a fire, PO, a bloody fire!'

He peered over the hatching, confirming my suspicions. 'So there is; looks like it's the engine room. Calm down, young un, stokers will be taking care of it.'

We sailed back down the Thames with remnants of smoke leaking from the vents. What little hair I'd had on my lower legs was singed off, but, fortunately, my trousers remained serviceable—so did the engines.

The DTS sailed across the North Sea to Germany, taking advantage of the Kiel Canal's short cut into the Baltic Sea.

The Navy could be a strange and unfathomable service at times: I'd been given two days stoppage of pay and leave—the leave part meaning the next two days.

The pay was a straightforward matter, but the leave? Still remains puzzling. Even though we were in the middle of the North Sea, I still had to report to the officer of the watch at 17.00 and 21.00 hours, confirming my presence onboard and that I'd not sneaked ashore—adhering to my punishment. Maybe if I didn't report my presence there would be an immediate stocktaking of the ship's boats.

After safely navigating the canal, the squadron berthed in a crowded Kiel harbour. We moored alongside a German destroyer that was itself moored to another German destroyer. Going ashore was difficult, what with negotiating various tripping hazards and having to salute more times since I'd left Ganges.

We sailed through the Baltic, on our way to Stockholm, playing games with Russian intelligence-gathering ships disguised as trawlers.

We would make lists and detailed drawings of fantastical weapons and equipment we didn't have—the leading cook even wrote menus that would satisfy the requirements of a royal banquet—and throw them overboard with the gash, knowing full-well that the Russian's would salvage and go through it, looking for any information that might prove useful.

We wished them good luck with that.

After delivering much goodwill to Stockholm we turned round and delivered the same amount to Copenhagen. We went the long way back to the North Sea, sailing up and around Denmark, and then headed back to Devonport.

Having now been relieved of my butcher duties, I was required as a watch keeper. Even though lack of sleep was a nuisance, I enjoyed the middle and morning watches.

On lookout duty, on clear and starry nights, particularly in calm seas, there was a feeling of peaceful reassurance as the Torquay parted seas that seemed aware of its HMS, regal presence.

The North Sea could be, and often was, a stormy place with sea spray lashing the upper deck, so my favourite watch-keeping station in such weather conditions was in the wheelhouse. Better to be down there in the warm and dry rather than bridge-wing or quarterdeck lookout.

In most ships at that time, the wheelhouse was situated very near the centre of a ship. So even though you were steering, you couldn't see where you were going.

I can vividly remember my first time on the wheel after previous hours spent in the wheelhouse—just observing.

'You ready, young un?' asked the quartermaster, a leading seaman called Harry Higgs, known as Big H. 'You know what to say?'

'Yes, Hooky, I think so.'

'Best hope you do, then.' He clicked down the tannoy button and called the bridge: 'Bridge, wheelhouse.'

After a moment came the reply: 'Bridge.'

'Permission for Junior Seaman Neylan to take the wheel, sir.'

'Is that my new gunner?' replied the Gunnery Officer, obviously Officer of the watch.

'That's him, sir,'

'Give him the wheel but keep a ruddy eye on him—there's a lot of traffic about. And make sure he's not chasing the ruddy lubber's line!'

I gingerly stepped behind the large wooden wheel. 'Bridge, wheelhouse,'

'Bridge,'

'Junior Seaman Neylan on the wheel, sir. Both engines half ahead, revolutions nine zero, course to steer one, seven, five, sir.'

'Very good. Be ready for course changes; it's like Piccadilly Circus out there.'

146

'Aye, aye, sir.'

I managed the course changes, with Big H's guiding hand on the wheel and, this being part of the excellent training I received on the Torquay, soon became a competent helmsman.

The wheelhouse, being located off the main passageway, was a focal point for ratings popping in for a natter—it was a good place for catching up with the latest ship's gossip.

I'd started my gunnery training by being deployed to the gun bay. Midway between the magazine and the twin turret, the gun bay received ammunition from the magazine below, and sent it up to the turret by way of a hydraulic hoist system. The system had to be maintained and I was taught how to do it, albeit only requiring my familiarisation with a grease gun.

After a few months of that I was moved up and into the turret, on the port gun. It's just about impossible to describe the inside of a turret and the loading of guns, but I'll try.

To the left, in front of the port gun breach, was the loading tray. Opposite the tray were two hoists: one for the cartridge, the other the shell. One gunner stood at the side of the tray and in front of the cartridge hoist, the other in front of him and facing the shell hoist. By just a swivel of the hips the cartridge was pulled from the hoist and placed on the tray. Similarly the shell was placed in front of the cartridge, immediately followed by the shell-loader hitting the breach handle. The tray would then roll over in line with the breach and the ammunition rammed into it. The breach closed, received a firing pulse, and fired. The recoil ejected the empty cartridge, triggered a blast of compressed air to clear the barrel of burnt cordite, opened the breach, rolled the loading tray back over and the whole process began again.

It all happened very quickly, very quickly indeed, and the two loaders would be (should be) waiting with cartridge and shell before the tray rolled back.

The noise was incredible. The gun firing was barely audible inside the confined space of the turret - it was the noise of the ramming, then the recoil, coupled with the noise of the machinery making it all happen that made the most noise.

The Captain of the gun sat in a little cage, above and between the guns. After the initial 'commence firing, load, then shoot', he would be screaming instructions that would never be heard, not even by himself—relying on his waving of arms—until all firing had ceased.

Contrary to what is seen and heard in many war films concerning the Royal Navy in action, the command to actually fire the guns was 'shoot'. Harking back to when ships were made of wood and 'fire' could easily be misinterpreted as an actual fire – somewhere.

An accepted rate of fire was supposed to be between six and seven rounds a minute, per gun. That rate was never achieved when I moved from loading cartridges to loading shells.

The cartridges weighed about sixteen pounds, so I managed okay. The shells, however, weighed about fifty-two pounds. I managed about five rounds a minute shooting at aircraft, but dropping to a woeful three or four if we were shooting at a surface target.

During anti-aircraft shooting, the gun barrel, obviously, was raised, meaning that the breach end lowered, which was easier for loading. With the barrel horizontal, firing at surface targets, I had to lift the shell to shoulder height before dropping it onto the tray—I just wasn't built for it. Coupled with that was the fear of incorrectly pulling the shell from the hoist. If you did it wrong then the shell below the one you were pulling out would come shooting up, and it wasn't opposed to mangling fingers that got in its way.

My limitations were duly and publicly noted.

My next move was into the gun's captain position. That was easy enough: somebody shouted in my earphones and I would shout exactly the same to the gun crew, even though I knew they couldn't hear me. When I heard 'check, check, check', I would repeat it, screaming as loud as I could and waving my arms. That was the verbal signal for the crew to stop loading, which was a bit of nonsense for one of the guns because the firing pulse would have been stopped and they couldn't very well load a gun that was already loaded.

But then my big moment would come—when others could actually hear me.

In front of me was a panel of lights, indicating the state of the guns after 'check, check, check'. I read them and repeated what they said to the Gun Direction Platform. It was usually 'both guns empty', or left/right gun empty, left/right gun loaded. Ideally, the two guns were never left in a loaded state at the same time. The recoil from a broadside (both guns firing at the same time) could do some serious damage to all kinds of delicate machinery and weapons systems, and seriously pee off the crew.

Having experienced my gunnery baptism, which was similar to Ganges training - thrown in at the deep end - I returned to my initial action station in the gun bay. I wasn't about to dispute the decision—not at all. I was also pleased when the Gunnery Officer informed me that I'd earned my Seaman Gunners Star, which I'd receive when I became an Ordinary Seaman. Marvellous!

On the 21st of July 1970, the Torquay sailed into Chatham Dockyard for a refit. All accumulated junk and obsolete fittings and fixtures were removed, and either stored or taken to the dockyard scrap yard.

There was a townie of mine onboard; a Raleigh trained ordinary seaman from Edlington, called Ronny Adams—nicknamed Bonny Ronny, even though he had a face that wasn't about to launch a thousand ships.

On one fine and hot sunny day, Ronny and I were detailed to accompany a loaded flatbed truck, full of junk, to the scrap yard and unload it. Taking the opportunity to try and recover our much faded Mediterranean tan, we took off shirt and cap then sweated our way through unloading.

Job done, we donned shirts, secured the tailgate, and then informed the 'not-my-job-mate' driver that we were ready to return.

'Not according to me list - next job sail room, sez ere.'

'Come on, mate,' said Ronny, 'not far out of your way.'

'No it aint, not really, but walk will do you good, being stuck on a ship and all that. Look on it as a favour from me to you.'

'Sod off, then, yer miserable git.'

So he did.

As the truck trundled down the roadway I had a sudden feeling of being improperly dressed, felt my head, then realised our caps were still on the back of the truck.

150

'Bloody hell, Ronny, our caps—they're on the back of that bloody truck.'

Ronny's confirming hand flew to his head. 'That arsehole, that lazy sod; if he'd given us a lift...'

'Well he didn't, and he's buggered off; just hope we don't run into anybody who's likely to give us a bollocking...'

'Yeah, and report us to the 'swain. Keep your eyes skinned, Lofty.'

Pity I couldn't see round corners.

We set off on our long 'doing us good' walk back to the Torquay, stopping every now and then for a quick, hidden fag, scouting our way behind and ahead for any signs of authority.

Confident, with not far to go, we rounded a corner and were met by a wave of gold braid. With nowhere to hide we waited for the wave to break and dash us on the rocks of punishment.

We couldn't believe our eyes: walking straight towards us, flanked by two admirals, with a flotilla of gold braid protecting his stern, was the Prince of Wales.

I recognised him instantly: only last July all of Ganges had to crowd into rooms that had a television to watch his investiture.

Ronny and I frantically tried to merge into the background, any background, but the only merging option was a jump into the harbour, so we stood to one side, hoping that the Prince and his entourage would find acknowledging the presence of two lowly subordinates beneath them, and ignore us.

Some hope.

Unbelievably it was the Prince who spoke to us: 'Ah, two ratings without caps. What ship?' He didn't wait for an answer. 'I would know if you were wearing caps. You should be wearing caps. Where are they?'

My thinking was to just say we lost them and wait for the consequences. Not so Ronny: in full saluting mode he went full

151

tilt into a much too detailed and defensive account. At least he managed to include HMS Torquay during his explanation.

'Mmmm,' was the Prince's response, 'don't think you'll be getting those back in a hurry. Would be prudent if you both returned to your ship and found replacements.'

And with that he walked off. Our only punishment was being glared at by his gold-braided entourage.

'Crikey, Lofty, I didn't know whether to bow, kneel, say your highness, your worthiness or what.'

.'You did go on a bit; he was probably wishing he'd never bothered with us. But you did well, Ronny.'

'Yeah, but I don't think anybody will believe us.'

'Best keep it quiet, then. Word gets back to the 'swain and, well... you know...'

'Yeah, best do that.'

I've retold that story many times, to those who'd listen, and, admittedly, had a mixed belief or disbelief response. But it is true—ask Prince Charles.

Two months later, with the Torquay in the hands of the dockyard mateys, most of the remaining crew received their draft chits. I was heading for the delights of Rosyth, in Scotland, to join HMS Gurkha.

HMS Gurkha

HMS Gurkha was one of seven Tribal Class, Type 81 frigates, conceived from an idea in the 1950's and built in the early 1960's.

They were the first Royal Navy warships to be powered by a combined steam and gas turbine, which required two funnels - one for the steam machinery and the other for the gas turbine. The gas turbine enabled the ship to be ready for sailing in minutes; steam alone required hours.

One odd design decision was to fit Type 81's with only one propeller. Some commentators say it was to cut costs but, whatever the reason, one propeller led to limited manoeuvrability, especially when mooring. It also added to the misery of seasickness suffers in heavy seas.

Nevertheless Tribal's were impressive-looking warships that exemplified the power and strength of the Royal Navy.

Armament:

Two single-barrelled, shield- sided (open) 4.5inch guns (one forrard, one aft).

Two single-barrelled Bofors.

Two single-barrelled Oerlikons (mounted on the bridge wings).

Two four-rail Sea Cat missile launchers.

One triple-barrelled ASW mortar.

There was also a Westland Wasp helicopter which sat in a small hanger. The hanger deck would be raised so it became the taking off and landing platform.

Because the Tribal's main deployment area would be in the Far East and West Indies, they were fitted with full air conditioning. This could be inverted to combat the cold of Arctic conditions, although, in my experience, it couldn't even combat the cold of a Rosyth winter.

HMS Gurkha
North Sea 1972. Taken from Wasp helicopter as a souvenir for the visiting twenty Gurkha soldiers we had onboard, and the crew.

The Rosyth shore establishment, HMS Cochrane, had taken over administration of Gurkha as she undertook her lengthy refit. It was to there I reported in late September 1970.

Not yet commissioned, and having her final checks, it was deemed that juniors, like me, would only get in the way. So I messed in Cochrane in a mess not dissimilar to the one at Cambridge; and there were only two of us in it.

With Cochrane not really wanting anything to do with me, or having nothing for me to do, I loafed about for a week—just waiting.

I finally received orders to join the Gurkha—so off I went.

Gurkha wasn't that much larger than the Torquay. But with a more efficient propulsion arrangement, one propeller, and below deck design, she certainly appeared to be much larger. And much larger she had to be, with fifty more crew and a detachment of Royal Marines to quarter.

She also had a small NAAFI shop, run by a civilian, and a Chinese laundry crew that lived and laundried somewhere in the bowls of the ship.

And—only bunks—no hammocks!

Once again I was in the forrard seamen's mess, with messmates, all gunners, you could only wish for.

They were mostly of Scottish or Geordie origin, so were very quick-witted, funny and a few of them quite mad! My 'Lofty' nickname hadn't travelled with me, but for some reason

I could never fathom 'Nick Nick' was briefly given me as a nickname. 'Yorkie' wasn't an option because there was already a 'Yorkie' on board, and a leading seaman at that, so I was usually known, thankfully, as Chris.

Very early in January 1971 Gurkha, having been released by the dockyard fitters, left Rosyth and sailed down to Portland for its dreaded 'work up'- a newly commissioned ship and her crew had to prove to the powers that be that she was capable of meeting operational standards—high operational standards.

Proof was how we defended against submarine, airborne, and surface vessel attacks, and how we delivered our own attacks against the same.

Attacking was fairly straight forward—being attacked definitely wasn't. You could be anywhere on board when some manically infected CPO – they were mostly CPO's – would throw a smoke grenade and shout 'FIRE, FIRE, FIRE!' Or be watch on deck when 'man overboard' was piped through the tannoys. And we had to deal with all similar scenarios efficiently and effectively. We all lived on our nerves for nearly two months.

On one particular morning we were being attacked by efficiently annoying Buccaneers. They could fly very low under radar and were screaming overhead before you knew it.

I was on the gun direction platform, shouting out, to no one in particular, information that came through my headphones when a Buccaneer screamed overhead. In its wake followed a maniacal CPO screaming: 'BOMB BURST, BOMB BURST!' and activating a smoke grenade.

I was one of the personnel who he deemed had paid the ultimate price in defence of Queen and country, so I crawled under the GDP coving, remembering the pie I'd bought from the NAAFI earlier that morning (I was always hungry) that was tucked inside my foul-weather jacket. I was enjoying my pie when an angry face thrust itself into mine:

'IS THAT A PIE?'

'Err, yes, chief.'

'DEAD MEN DON'T EAT PIES!' I thought he'd shouted 'dead men don't tell lies'.

'It is a pie, chief, from the NAAFI, I bought it this morning.'

'WHAT THE...'

'He's a junior seaman, chief,' interrupted someone, his tone of voice suggesting a reminder of the limitations of junior seamen.

Just a few days later, on January 18th, having reached the grand age of 17 years and 6 months, the gunnery officer promoted me to Ordinary Seaman—a rank still bestowed with limitations—and also presented me with my cross-barrelled, one star, gunnery badges.

Of course I was delighted with my badge presentation, but my delight was somewhat subdued when I was told to have the badges sewn onto my various items of uniform within one week.

Marvellous!

After satisfying the Admiralty chappies that we had achieved operational status—to a very high standard—we left Portland for Portsmouth, where we rearmed, refuelled, and re-established our nerves.

All talk was of our impending visit to Amsterdam. Seasoned crew were only too willing to share lurid tales of this Dutch city, and I was looking forward to the visit—until...

The cox's'n summoned me to his office and told me that, no, I wasn't in trouble; none that he'd yet detected, anyway, and informed me that before I'd joined Gurkha I should have had some leave. With the beckoning delights of Amsterdam fully occupying my immature thoughts, I said it didn't matter, only to be told that it did matter and reminded that even the Chinese laundry crew had more say in what happened in my Navy life than I did.

Middle East Deployment

I returned from leave, closing my ears to all comments regarding Amsterdam.

We spent the following few months protecting survey ships in the English Channel and taking part in joint exercises off Scotland.

After a short visit to Newcastle we returned to Rosyth to refuel, store ship, and give those crew onboard who had married quarters there, time with their families before we started our nine-month deployment to the Middle East. Similarly, on our way to the Middle East, we docked in Portsmouth to allow others their visits, albeit only a week-end pass was granted.

On May 18th 1971 we departed Portsmouth and, via Gibraltar and St Helena, made our way down the west coast of Africa to Simonstown, in South Africa.

We crossed the equator on the first of June 1971 as we made our way down the coast of Africa. With much ceremony (mainly being doused with all manner of vegetable waste, mixed with seawater) I was received into the domain of the Dwellers of the Deep.

Simonstown was nothing much more than a port; but just a relatively short train ride away was Cape Town—a beautiful city—but imbued with South Africa's apartheid regime.

Apartheid wasn't a term I'd come across, but it became all too familiar in Cape Town. A few old hands had warned us 'young uns' what to expect and, 'just put up with it. It's their way... nothing to do with us.' Well, 'their way,' certainly wasn't my way, even after what followed a few days later.

Clive Reed was a black school-mate of mine. He lived near the secondary school we went too, and after school I would regularly walk with him to his house and wait inside whilst he changed. As I waited his mum would give me a cup of tea, often accompanied by a bun or slice of cake.

The colour of his skin was never an issue; nobody at school remarked on it, even after the infamous 'Rivers of Blood' speech—he was a friend, nothing more and nothing less.

I didn't see much of Clive when I went home on leave - he'd gone 'down south' to stay with an uncle and seek his fortune. He did return, without a fortune, and the last time I saw him he was the proud owner of a used-record shop on the outskirts of town, bought with his redundancy money from British Coal.

All across the city were signs saying 'Whites Only,' or, very rarely, 'Blacks Only.' They could be found on streets, footpaths, and entrances to shops, restaurants, or bars—almost everywhere people went about their daily lives.

On runs ashore in Cape Town we would go into establishments that had plush seating at polished tables and bars. At the far end of many a long, polished bar would be a head-height hole in the wall, facing it a black barman, or woman, who would serve the blacks, and blacks only, who were queuing outside. And they were served their drinks in glasses, cups, or jugs they'd brought themselves.

It was an incredibly sad state of affairs but, thank goodness, apartheid is buried in the past.

In Cape Town one night, leaving our final bar of the evening and heading for the train station, we became aware of being followed by a crowd of young black men. We'd been warned that street robbery was a Cape Town problem, but, especially being in uniform and quite a few of us, we'd never given a moment's thought of it happening to us. But it was—

more young men, shouting threats and demanding money, were waiting for us as we approached the station.

Somebody shouted, 'back-to-back lads, they'll soon bugger off!'

But they didn't.

I made sure I went back-to-back with Dave Dunne, a former Field Gunner, built like a brick out house. But even he couldn't save me, or himself—we were vastly outnumbered.

My last conscious sight, in the midst of all the kicking, thumping, and shouting, was the end of an iron bar being thrust towards my face. Thinking at least to save my teeth, I opened my mouth. Then I was out—out cold.

I came to and found myself leaning against the knees of a man I didn't know. Feeling groggy and confused I was, ludicrously, deciding whether or not to compliment him on his shiny shoes.

'It's okay, biddy, they won't be back,' said the stranger. Something caught the corner of my eye. I glanced to my left and saw him holding a huge handgun. A handgun that was very close to my left cheek. I passed out again.

I came to in hospital. A nurse was cleaning blood from my face with Dave Dunne and Jock Kirk looking on.

'I never thought you could get any uglier,' said Dave.

'Aye, he was never a hit with the lassies; blown his chances now,' said Jock, more than willing to add further words of consolation.

I couldn't reply because my mouth was full of wadding; but it didn't stop me trying.

'Shush now,' said the nurse. 'The roof of your mouth is damaged and a few teeth are loose. Are these two supposed to be your friends?' I just nodded.

'Oh, yes, we're a happy ship,' the cox's'n had arrived. 'And the Captain will be more than happy to see you three. Can I take them home?'

Eventually a doctor gave us the all clear, recommending we keep an eye on 'the little one'. Thanks, Doc.

Captain McKeown wasn't unsympathetic: 'It's my understanding that you had no choice but to defend yourselves—am I right?'

'We weren't looking for trouble, sir,' said Jock, 'they came out of nowhere.'

'Quite,' said the Skipper. 'A bloody good job that off-duty policeman came to your rescue or I might have had to leave here with a reduced crew, and bothering myself with writing to your loved ones, if you have any.'

'Ordinary Seaman Neylan?'

The wadding had been removed by the leading medical assistant. 'Yes, sir?'

'I do believe you were late on board. Three hours adrift.'

'Sorry, sir, but...'

'Given the circumstances I'll overlook it this time.'

That was good of him.

'Be warned, all of you, and spread the word—going ashore and looking for some kind of retribution will not be tolerated—am I clear?'

We delivered a unified 'Aye, aye, sir.'

'Any trouble, any trouble at all tonight will result in all shore leave being cancelled. Dismissed.'

The cox's'n gathered us in his office. 'Due to your injuries' - Jock had a broken finger; Dave a nasty cut on his head - 'you're all medically unfit to go ashore until the LMA says so. But, like the skipper said: no retribution. Spread the word.'

'Bloody hell, 'swain,' said Jock, 'it was a street brawl, not bloody Rorke's Drift.'

'I know, but give me just one chance to kick your arses, and I will.'

The roof of my mouth cleared up but I would have problems with my teeth for many years to come.

Just before we slipped from Simonstown, heading for a spell on Beira patrol, I was called into the writers' office.

The Purser (or Pusser) was the ship's banker, so to speak. He ordered and paid for stores etc. He also paid the crew.

Onboard Gurkha he had a writer as his assistant: an obnoxious individual who thought more about himself than anyone else ever would. I was told to pay him a visit.

'We've received a bill from Cape Hospital for your treatment,' was the greeting I received. 'Comes to just over £100, in old money.'

'What!'

Clearly satisfied he'd caused some distress, he added more: 'You can pay it off at, let's say, ten bob a week.'

'Ten bob!'

'Thought that might come as a shock, but don't worry your little self, the Navy will pay your bill. Don't get into any more fights because we might not be so generous next time.'

We? I won't, arsehole. And I bet you're not brave enough to say the same to Dave and Jock. He must have read my mind: 'Bugger off.'

For complicated political reasons Rhodesia (now Zimbabwe) had been blockaded by the British Government. The Royal Navy was tasked with blockading the port of Beira, where most of Rhodesia's imported oil was delivered by—tanker.

The Navy's task was to deter said tankers from entering Beira, with force, if need be. The reality was that using force was, in itself, a complicated affair. Permission had to be sought to threaten force, then more permission to activate it. To further complicate matters, what force to use had to be debated by our government. What a mess, what nonsense.

The leading hand of the gunners mess, Phil Green, was full of common sense:

'If we did blow a tankers steering to bits, then we would, as the nearest ship, be required by maritime law to take it in tow to the nearest port. And that port being Beira... well...'

We didn't come across any blockade-running tankers—what nonsense.

We spent a monotonous month patrolling the sea off Beira. The monotony only broken by RAF Shackleton's dropping our mail and the obligatory kite flying and tug 'o' war contests.

We only had the one kite flying contest because the stokers mess decided to build a kite out of two painting stages (long wooden planks used for sitting on when painting the ship's side) and blankets. When they launched it off a platform, just below the bedstead radar, it spiralled down and just missed two sub-lieutenants who were launching their own, conventionally-built kite.

The tug 'o' war didn't fare much better. How could a team possibly hope to get away with tying the end of their rope to a stanchion, or belaying it around a bollard? Jolly Jack Tars—at their best.

It was during the patrol that the Gunnery Officer, Bumble - he did look like Dickens' Mr Bumble - took me for my able seaman exam. Thanks to the specialised crew on the Torquay, and the Gurkha fo'c'sle men—especially Pete Green and John Lilly (who was an expert in all things relating to anchor work and cables)—I passed.

I've often wondered how much gash there must have been on the bottom of that patrol area after so many years— especially the amount of empty beer cans.

In the middle of July 1971 we sailed into Mombasa and, having reached age eighteen, my shore leave was extended to the same as everybody else's.

Mombasa was where we had our rest and recreation time. Some had a short stay at the Golden Sands holiday beach resort; others went on mini safaris and quite a few trawled the bustling markets, buying wood carvings from the many souvenir stalls. I do believe that even if we lost our keel, the Gurkha would have remained afloat, kept buoyant by the amount of carvings that were amassed by the crew.

As was my way, I was content to just laze about and enjoy the rest.

The final days of July found Gurkha patrolling the Persian Gulf, policing the Massendam Peninsula, looking for contraband hidden onboard the many Dhows that frequented it. A task, thankfully, borne by the Royal Marines detachment.

We then joined a few US Navy ships for joint-training exercises. One part of the training was using main armament to destroy shore targets.

The Yanks had placed various large vehicles (old lorries, fuel tankers etc.) on the beach of a small uninhabited island, which would be our targets.

The US Navy sailed past, all guns blazing, and didn't hit a thing.

The Gurkha launched its Wasp helicopter as a spotter for our two 4.5inch guns. We sailed past the island and, after a few ranging shots, turned the vehicles into so much scrap yard junk.

'That's how you do it,' beamed Bumble. 'Watch and learn, watch and learn!' he shouted to the US Navy as we showed them our stern, leaving the exercise, bound for Bahrain.

We spent a self-maintenance week in Bahrain and that, for the seamanship branch, meant chipping, scraping and painting the superstructure. We were, after all, flying the flag and reminding those that needed reminding, that Great Britain was still a powerful force. And having a sparkly clean warship was all part and parcel of it all.

We left Bahrain in early October and called in at Bandar Abbas, in Iran, where the Royal Marine's provided a guard to salute one of their highest ranking admirals.

Colombo, in Ceylon (now Sri Lanka) was the next place to be shown the White Ensign before we joined a small fleet of Royal Navy ships commemorating some historic event off the coast of Singapore.

The fleet, lead by the aircraft carrier HMS Eagle, then commenced exercises in the Malacca Strait. After so long sailing alone, it was reassuring being in company with other Royal Navy ships. It was also beneficial—the Eagle had its own bakery, which the small ships took full advantage of.

On completion of the exercise we put into Penang for a short visit before moving on to Singapore for yet another bout of ship maintenance and recreation.

Recreation time was mostly spent in the numerous bars and hotels in and around Bugis Street. Not as busy and vibrant an area as it once was, I was told, because of the recent withdrawal of British troops.

It was in early December that war broke out between Pakistan and India, and the Gurkha was ordered to sail to the warzone in the Bay of Bengal to assist in any rescue and evacuation of British nationals caught up in the conflict.

We might have to defend ourselves against any of the two armed forces who considered we favoured one over the other, so we swapped all of our practise ammunition for live and crammed as many extra rounds as we could onboard. And, to minimise the risk of being mistaken for the enemy, we had huge Union Jacks painted on the upper deck flat surfaces, and flew so many Jacks, ensigns, and pennants, it appeared that we were having our own fleet review.

Once in the Bay of Bengal we assumed defence stations: alternating port and starboard six hour watches—half the ship's company closed up, the other half eating or sleeping.

This proved to have a considerable impact on body clocks: sometimes we'd come off watch, have a shower, turn in, turn out and be fed. Other times we'd come off watch, be fed, have a shower, turn in then turn out straight back on watch. After a few days of this we'd never quite know what meal to look forward to: sometimes we'd turn in after a breakfast; other times we'd turn out and have a dinner—very confusing. Then everything would change if an unknown ship or aircraft pinged the defence radar. Action stations would sound and we'd all be closed up!

We weren't attacked, didn't rescue or evacuate anyone, and only rescued from the monotony of defence stations when we were eventually stood down.

The Seychelles were our next destination and we were looking forward to spending Christmas in, the old hands said, a tropical paradise. On the way there I would be taken back in time by thoughts of the Screamer at Ganges.

On board Gurkha was a particularly obnoxious junior stoker called Smarty Smithson, who had an over-inflated opinion of himself. He did like to think he was smart so liked his nickname; but he had no idea of the irony that lay behind it because Smarty wasn't smart, or clever—he was thick, and irritatingly so. He thought it clever to butt in and voice his opinion on issues he knew nothing about. Thought it clever and funny to completely immerse the ladle in the gravy urn, and tell the leading chef he would never be as good a cook as his mother. He was the epitome of stupid and childish.

I'd just finished the first watch (20:00 to 00:00) in the wheelhouse and was making my way forrard through the galley flat when I thought I heard screaming. I had, it was coming from the scullery, next to the galley. But I was puzzled: the scullery door was never closed, except when we closed up at action or defence stations.

Jimmy Cook, a leading stoker, appeared. 'Ah, good, he's still screaming,' said Jimmy.

'Who's still screaming, and why's he screaming? What's going on, Jimmy?'

'It's Smarty; teaching him a lesson. Tied him to the deck in there. By the sounds of it I don't think he likes cockroaches overmuch.'

'Bloody hell, Jimmy, that's a bit much, don't you think?'

'Don't you think he deserves it? Time we taught him a lesson?'

'Well... there is that, I suppose, but what if the OOTW or somebody else comes by and hears him?'

'Cleared it from the top, Chris, lad. Cleared it from the top. You turning in or skiving?'

'Turning in.'

'Off you go, then. We'll let him out soon.'

'Well I hope it works, Jimmy, I really do, but bloody hell...'

'Yeah, so say all of us.'

It did work: Smarty was a changed young man. The stokers even considered changing his nickname to Goody. But they never did.

171

The Seychelle Islands were, indeed, a group of tropical paradise islands.

Myself and some others from the mess befriended a retired librarian who we met on the local beach. A Seychelles holiday had been her main retirement present. She'd been the boss in some important library in London and was very posh—but not standoffish. We included her in our runs ashore and, when we were messing about on the beach, even helped with her attempts at learning to swim. She demonstrated her thanks by buying us Christmas dinner, well, turkey salad, at a beach restaurant, which we ate sitting amongst the shade-giving sand dunes.

Our next stop was Mauritius, where we were quickly barred from the RAF base canteen and bar for being too rowdy and too liberal with bad language. But that barring drove us to celebrate the new year of 1972 at the few beach bars there were—the owners more than willing to take our money no matter how rowdy we were, or uncouth our language became.

We sailed back to Rosyth via the outward route we'd taken, and arrived home in early February 1972. On the way home, on the 18th of January, I was promoted to Able Seaman.

Marvellous!

During March of that year we spent most of our time involved with NATO exercises in the North Sea. Bumble had decided it a good opportunity for me to become familiar with our unique 4.5inch shield-sided, open guns.

During the exercises John Lilly was captain of 'A' gun, situated just aft of the fo'c'sle. 'Y' gun was at the stern (don't ask). And it was John's task to familiarise me with the gun, kicking my arse when appropriate.

An open gun was much easier to load than a turreted gun: there were no finger-mangling ammunition hoists because a line of Bootnecks (Royal Marines) passed the ammunition from the ready-use magazine, located in the fo'c'sle flat. There was more room to move and not as much noise from hydraulic machinery; but we were poorly shielded from the noise of the gun firing.

However, in a turret, the gun crew, obviously, moved with the turret. At an open gun the crew (who were not important enough to be seated) had to move with the gun as it traversed— getting knocked over was both embarrassing and painful.

I'd told John about my experiences in the turret on the Torquay so, obviously, John being John, had me loading shell on the first surface-target shoot. Needless to say I was very relieved to hear 'check, check, check'; followed by John declaring 'A' gun empty.

'Hey, Nick Nick,' shouted John (he still used my mostly redundant nickname), 'Bumble isn't happy with our rate of fire. He's not a happy Bumble.'

'Yeah, well, make him happy and get *your* arse over here.'

'Tut, tut—that's no way to talk to the captain of the gun.'

'Well, if you're so important, make everybody happy and send us all to stand-easy.'

'Yeah, Royal Navy frigate lost cos Able Seaman Nick Nick on 'A' gun, a self-elected official of the Seafarers Union, demanded his right to a tea break. That should go down well with the Admiralty, yer silly sod.'

Bumble inadvertently intervened on my behalf. Announcing all guns cease fire—the shoot was over—he followed that instruction with another. Before sponging out and securing, both guns would be manually laid (aimed) at a French destroyer—Bumble's choice of surface target—to check the alliance with the automatic gun direction and aiming radar.

John moved me onto the gun-layers seat with an encouraging: 'hope the muscles in your eyes are bigger than the ones on your arms.'

Lining up the gun sights was relatively easy in a calm sea; almost impossible in a rough sea, so I was thankful for the calm weather that day. But not as thankful when John, putting me soundly in my place, took advantage of his role as the gun's captain to nominate me as one of the gunners who would be sponging out the barrel and securing 'A' gun.

Served me right, I suppose.

In early April we embarked twenty Gurkha soldiers, eager to sail in the ship named after them. To further enhance their Gurkha experience, we gave them passage to Southampton so they could visit the shipbuilding birthplace of the warship.

Whilst in Southampton a request was received from the WRNS for Gurkha to give a party of them the short passage to Portsmouth, where we would be disembarking the soldiers.

We made the mistake of leaving our spare caps unattended; leaving the WRNS with the opportunity to liberate the tallies from the caps they came across.

I wonder if mine's a proud possession somewhere.

West Indies

Back in Rosyth we had a small refit and maintenance period in preparation for our forthcoming deployment to the West Indies, sailing in early June.

However, the dockyard maties had a grievance with their employers and downed tools. The Gurkha was locked in her basin, freedom dictated by the maties, who stood their ground for five, long weeks.

All we could do was pass the time as pleasantly as we could: playing a lot of football and cricket and keeping well out of the way of the bo's'n.

During one football match I tackled and unintentionally broke a leg of Andy McDermott, a Killick TAS rating. Andy was married with children and lived in a Rosyth married quarter. After much swearing and recriminatory language Andy, although in agonising pain, managed to perceive a positive: he wouldn't be sailing with us to the Windies; his leg would be in plaster for quite a while and he'd have to spend time at home recuperating.

Some three months later, when Andy rejoined the Gurkha, he gave me a fiver as a thank you for breaking his leg. Every cloud...

Gunners mess football team, taken in Puerto Rico (1972) by John Lilly. I'm on the back row – third from the right.

In early July the maties approved our freedom and, after storing ship and calling in to Portsmouth to top up with ammunition, and a brief stop to refuel in the Azores, we sailed across the North Atlantic, bound for Bermuda.

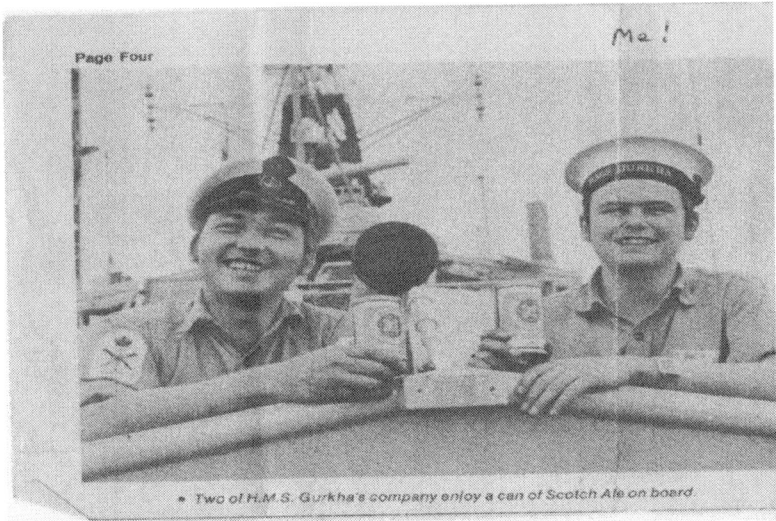

Ma!

* Two of H.M.S. Gurkha's company enjoy a can of Scotch Ale on board.

Taken just after completion of storing ship

The West Indies are, on the most part, a stunningly beautiful group of islands. We visited most of them and, unfortunately for the seaman branch, most had dignitaries, VIP's and public figures who, so thought the Navy, required indulging as a way to demonstrating Britain's friendly and cordial temperament.

The indulgences that affected the seaman branch were, mostly, the skipper and his officers hosting onboard soiree-like parties. This involved the seamanship branch having to rig awnings on upper deck spaces to protect guests from the glare of the sun or an evening shower. And they were a sod to rig—a right pain in the backside.

One such awning-rigging event in Barbados proved to be very irksome.

After much sweating, and muscle-wrenching awning rigging, John Lilly and I, looking forward to a stand-easy, were commandeered by a petty officer steward to collect spare tables and chairs from the wardroom stowage compartment, and move them to the upper deck.

After being deprived of a recuperative stand-easy, John and I we're not in the best of moods, so dragged rather than carried most of the furniture out of the compartment.

'Excuse me,' said a lower-rate steward, emerging from the wardroom, 'could you keep the noise down.' His tone suggested he was ordering, rather than requesting—a please would have helped—but not much.

'It's tables and chairs we're moving,' retorted John, 'not bloody cushions.'

'Well, you're making a lot of noise, and the gentlemen don't like to be disturbed by noise when they're off duty.'

'Gentlemen! Are you soddin joking?'

I could see that John was about to boil over—it didn't take much.

'Listen, mate,' I said, 'you go and look after your *gentlemen,* we're nearly done.'

'If you're so bloody worried about your *gentlemen,* why don't YOU chuffin move...'

Noticing steam coming from John's ears, the steward did the sensible thing and retreated to the wardroom.

I spent the rest of the day thanking the RN for my selection as a seaman—not as a steward—I don't think I could have lived with the shame.

Puerto Rico housed a large American base, and it was there that I discovered Americans did everything big. Their aircraft carriers could have swallowed two of ours; you could get lost in their bars and restaurants, and the majority of their cars would have failed to negotiate the streets of Doncaster.

Very soon after we'd berthed there were people streaming up the gangway, bombarding the Quartermaster with cards and leaflets, advertising everything from tailors to taxis. After a while the QM just opened the top of his lofty desk and gestured for the paraphernalia to be placed inside.

Except for the duty watchmen, we decided, as a mess, to go ashore that first evening and experience life the American way.

'You ready to go ashore, Chris lad?'

'Yeah, just about, hooky.'

'Off you go, then, and organise some fast blacks.'

'How many?'

'Best make it three,' said Pete Green after a quick headcount.

'Where to?'

'The PX base, or something like that. Just say PX, they'll know.'

So I made my way up to the gangway. 'Any taxi cards, Paddy?'

'There's a chuffin desk full, help yourself.' said the disgruntled QM.

I fished one out and used the newly-installed landline to dial a number the length of my arm.

'Hey, you dialled the exact correct number; where are you and where do you wanna go? No journey's too short or too long for Big City cabs.'

I was a bit taken aback by the spiel; 'Err... from HMS Gurkha and to... somewhere called the PX?'

'Are you the okay British ship that just landed?'

I thought the HMS bit might have been a bit of a give away, but... 'Yeah, that's the one.'

'How many for, buddy?'

'About twelve, best send...'

'You got yourself a Big City cab arriving in ten minutes. You be having yourselves a good time.'

'We need more than one...' But he'd rung off.

'Bloody hell, Paddy, he's only sending one, and most of the mess is going ashore.'

'Trust me, young un, from what I've seen, one'll be enough, sure it will.'

And he was right: I'd never seen such a large taxi.

We all rushed to board the very large fast black, that was, paradoxically, a big silver monster—only its tyres were black. And why did we rush? Because we wanted to avoid riding shotgun—the seat next to the driver.

Gurkha sailors had an unusual tradition regarding taxis. When a taxi arrived at its destination then, as was fair, all passengers contributed evenly to the fare. However, if the taxi was full enough to require someone riding shotgun, when it neared its destination and had to stop at traffic lights, or queue in traffic, the backseat passengers would bail out, leaving the shotgun passenger to pay the fare—without any contributions—when the taxi finally reached its destination. Those were the rules. 'Seeing red' had an altogether different meaning for a shotgun passenger.

No one rode shotgun that evening - the driver was cocooned in his own driving bubble.

We chose a restaurant in the PX complex, chose a large enough table and sat down, anticipating good service and appetizing food, based on the written promises made outside.

After browsing the menu I said I'd be ordering a T-bone steak, with chips, as you do, but a knowledgeable someone told me, well, all of us not versed in American cuisine, that chips were crisps and the chips we wanted were french-fries. Complicated.

My steak arrived—it was so large it could have doubled for a Sunday roast, even for a family as large as mine. Indeed, there would have been enough left over to feed the dog, if we had one. But I tackled it with gusto, only giving up when my arteries put in a formal complaint.

A waitress came to clear the table: 'My, you British boys sure know how to eat,' she said. 'I'll clear away and you be sure to let me know if you want dessert.'

'Pudding,' said Pete, noticing a few confused faces. 'Dessert is a pudding.'

An ever gallant Hamish Muir asked if she wanted any help: 'Oh, a British gentleman; but, no thanks, I'm good.'

'What's she good at?' said Hamish when the waitress had left with her first load.

'Clearing up, obviously, peg 'ead,' said Sammy Hoag.

John Lilly butted in: 'And an ugly sod like you won't ever find out what else she's good at.'

And that was the first Americanism I came across, and, I have to confess, I find them very irritating now that they've crossed the Atlantic—Let's do this, not on my watch, 24/7, don't do that already, no brainer, back in the day, hi, guys—and so on. But by far the worst must be 'no problem'. I don't expect 'a problem' when I'm in a bakers asking for a loaf, or asking for a menu in a restaurant.

Very irritating.

After a brief visit to Caracas in Venezuela, we spent the rest of our deployment exercising with war ships from different Caribbean countries.

The Dominican Republic Navy proved to be, well, fascinating. We were having a practise shoot at a towed surface target and, having made our firing pass, we waited for an old, recycled Dominican frigate to make hers.

After about fifteen minutes she managed to get off a round from one of her guns. Her crew were obviously thrilled with this achievement because there was much cheering and back-slapping all along the frigate's upper deck—even though that round had burst up in the clear, blue sky.

At the end of November 1972 we began our long voyage back across the Atlantic, finally reaching Rosyth in the middle of December.

After a much looked forward to and restful leave, in January of 1973 we left Rosyth to join with other NATO ships exercising in the east Atlantic. When the exercise ended we sailed for Lisbon and had, what turned out to be, a rowdy run ashore.

I can't remember what exactly happened, not being as sober as I ought to have been, except that George Pope and I found ourselves being hurled into the back of a Portuguese police car. As a policeman slammed the door shut, we scrambled across the back seats and exited by the other door, then ran all the way back to the Gurkha. Must be the shortest time two naval rating have spent in police custody.

Relieved at escaping Portuguese justice, unlike three unfortunate ratings from the after seaman's mess, I was happy to leave Lisbon and sail for Gibraltar.

There was a moment of panic, though, when I was summoned to the cox's'n's office. But I was relieved, although saddened, when he presented me with a draft chit.

The time had come, as I knew it would, for my status as Able Seaman to correspond with my gunnery qualifications. So I was off to HMS Excellent Gunnery School, in Portsmouth, to undertake a specialised gunnery course.

Bumble, probably because of my abysmal firing rate, had suggested I do the armourer's part of the Quarters Rate course, meaning I would be fixing guns, rather than loading them.

Thanks, Bumble.

However, with the gunnery course not starting until early April, the Navy, in their unfathomable wisdom, first sent me to Chatham to join HMS Triumph, a former aircraft carrier now being converted into a heavy repair ship. Why couldn't they find me a berth in Portsmouth instead of forcing me to lug my kit twice across half the country? I was only going to be with the Triumph for a month, for goodness sake.

I was sad to be leaving the Gurkha, mostly because of the good friendships I'd made. But also, because, in my opinion, the Tribal class frigates were the most impressive looking frigates ever to be built.

Conversely, I was very happy to be going home because I'd fallen in love with a lass in Doncaster. And, during my next leave, we'd be planning our wedding.

I flew back to the UK from Gibraltar; but not, thankfully, in a Britannia.

HMS Excellent

After spending my time on the Triumph, mostly unbolting bunks and placing them in storage, I joined Excellent on the fifth of April.

HMS Excellent sits on Whale Island in Portsmouth. The island originated from the muck and silt excavated when the dockyard was being built in the 19th century.

Apart from its responsibilities for all things gunnery, the gunnery branch of the Royal Navy are (or were) the marching experts. Indeed, you couldn't possibly be a parade-drill instructor and not be a gunner. This might have changed – I hope not.

Through the main gate and just in front of the guard room, was a large, glass cabinet that contained the gun carriage that had carried the late, great Sir Winston Churchill's coffin on his final journey. Every rating who drew that carriage was a gunner.

Excellent was also where the Navy's field gunners trained. Just above their training ground were the cricket pitches: a huge contrast between the shouting, swearing, grunting, and sweating of field gunners, as opposed to the genteel game of cricket.

Excellent, then, was in many ways like being back in Ganges. Parade drill was always an important element with any training undertaken there and, whilst other shore establishments had adopted a more relaxed version of morning divisions, Excellent's were rigorous to the point of being fanatical. The reasoning was, I suppose, that any Royal Navy ship, anywhere in the world, could rely on their gunnery ratings when undertaking ceremonial duties or providing guards of honour.

But their reliance on me was sorely tested onboard HMS Victory.

I married my fiancé whilst on leave just after joining Excellent, and we moved to live on the top floor of a house on Laburnum Grove, in Portsmouth's North End.

To save on bus fares I bought myself a bicycle in order to commute between home and Whale Island. My wife was an employee of Boots the chemists and had managed to get a transfer to their branch in North End.

So all the going was good. It became even better when I was given married quarters - a top floor maisonette on Finch Road in Eastney, which had a lovely view of the Solent, over to the Isle of Wight. My wife, however, endured the cost of bus travel rather than endure cycling across Portsmouth.

My gunnery course was going well—learning how to maintain and repair guns rather than loading them with heavy shells.

Ubiquitous parade drill was always prevalent, with learning more complex aspects of marching: slow march, changing formation etc and the more intricate aspects of marching with the SLR.

Nearing the end of our course my class was chosen to provide a guard of honour for a visiting French Admiral.

Possibly, as a gesture of 'let bygones be bygones', we would be providing the guard onboard HMS Victory, Lord Nelson's wooden flag ship at the battle of Trafalgar.

Not being a trusting lot, Excellent's instructors made sure the guard would be as smart as smart can be by providing us with sparkly white webbing, highly polished buckles and clasps, whiter than white white fronts and caps, and immaculately pressed collars and silks. Our boots, however, as dictated by Excellent, were always in a state of shiny readiness.

The problem started, well, my problem, when the heavens opened. Not wanting a visiting French admiral catching a cold, a British one, the guard would be presenting arms below decks.

Mustered in an old sail loft nearby Victory, with bayonets fixed, the CGI in charge had just enough time to drill us once on below-deck presenting arms. Needless to say, as at Ganges, I was in the middle of the front rank.

'Remember,' he shouted, 'over and down, right boot behind the left. DO NOT DO THE UP BIT! There's no room. If anybody's bayonet so much as scrapes Victory's deckhead—they'll wish they'd never been born!'

Having been inspected by the CGI and a flotilla of gold-braided uniforms, we marched up Victory's gangway and then made our way down to the lower gun deck; a feat in itself considering our SLR's still had bayonets fixed—the CGI didn't want our grubby hands spoiling his shiny bayonets.

I hadn't been aboard the Victory before and was completely overawed by the size of the massive 32-pounder canon on the lower gun deck—lined up in front of their gun ports.

We mustered in threes, dressed, stood at ease, and waited.

The CGI took his cue from a gunnery officer waiting at the bottom of a ladder: 'Victory guard... guard... HO!' We sprang to attention. To our front strode a figure dressed in a dazzling green uniform I'd never seen the likes of before. He turned and stood facing us, blocking my view of the canon.

'Guard... general salute... present—arms!'

Still overawed I completely forgot about the below-deck drill.

Over... two three... up... two three... down. I heard suppressed sniggers as my bayonet thrust into the deckhead. And it remained fixed despite my desperate attempts to pull it free. The CGI strode forward and looked me straight in the eye. Mouthing 'you bleedin idiot,' he wrapped two huge fists around my bayonet handle and yanked it free.

For the rest of the week, whilst the rest of my class enjoyed their stand-easy, I doubled around Excellent's huge parade ground.

Served me right, I suppose.

I've been to visit Victory quite a few times over the years, vainly searching for a bayonet-shaped blemish in the deckhead of the lower gun deck.

With our enhanced gunnery course now coming to its conclusion, we were sent to HMS Phoenix to complete the obligatory fire-fighting and damage control course that followed almost every Royal Navy course.

Phoenix was a shore establishment which was situated a short march from Excellent. But, I believe, it has now become part of it.

Apart from the admin buildings, Phoenix was a collection of large metal containers, replicating ship compartments.

Dressed in overalls we would enter a container and tackle whatever was thrown at us. Some would have water gushing in from various holes in the deckhead, deck and bulkheads (walls). We would vainly attempt to plug the leaks by hammering different shapes and sizes of wood into them. If - a big if - we managed to plug all the holes, others would open up. We never did win.

Other compartments would fill with fire and smoke as soon as we'd entered them. We quickly learnt to find and make good use of the fire-fighting equipment before the smoke and heat became too intense. To add to the enjoyment there were very heavy sand-filled dummy casualties to be rescued.

What I found bizarre was, after we'd dragged out the casualties and were released from rescuing duties, most fell on the grass outside, coughing and choking, whilst reaching for their fags. Yes—I was one of them.

Final Draft Chit

On the 20th of July 1973 I was awarded my QR2 gun badges. Soon after that I received another draft chit.

The Gods had truly smiled on me because I was to remain at Excellent, though based out at Fraser gunnery range, in Eastney, just ten minutes walk from my married quarter.

Smashing!

Fraser was reached via a long driveway off Cumberland road. To the right of the driveway, before the Solent, was scrubland. To the left was a large tarmac area where motorcycle display teams sometimes practised. And just before the gate (a barrier, really) and guard room was a small football pitch with just one set of goalposts.

Fraser had an array of guns, missile launchers and target-finding radar, all pointing out into the Solent. One of those guns was a 4.5inch open gun—exactly the same as the two on the Gurkha.

My job was maintaining this gun and assisting with training ratings and officers who had a draft chit to join a Tribal class frigate—most of them unfamiliar with this type of gun. In charge of me was Dave Mann, a Chief Electrical/Mechanical Engineer.

Apart from the gun, we were responsible for repairing and maintaining two different sized, heavy-gauge metal, rolling platforms. These were platforms that could tilt and roll, used for sea-testing machinery and various kinds of armament. Because maximum load warnings were frequently ignored, we tended to fix them more than maintain them.

Fraser would empty during the early evening as loaded busses returned staff and trainees to their sleeping quarters in Excellent. Those, like me, based at Fraser, followed a ship's watch keeping system during Fraser's non-training times.

We spent most of the time sitting in the guard room. If it wasn't cold or raining, or the Officer of the Watch was about, we would occasionally venture out to check that no one had stolen a missile launcher or Bofors gun. And, of course, we would always be pandering to the whims of Rufus, Fraser's adopted dog.

Life was good, very good.

Annexed to Fraser was HMS St George—a training school mostly for senior ratings who had come up through the ranks and been promoted to officer status.

I was on my way back from HMS Sultan, having been reduced to begging for spare parts for our rolling platforms. As I passed St George I bumped into Pete Green, my former boss, mentor, and good friend from HMS Gurkha, dressed in a Sub-Lieutenants uniform.

'You still giving all you have to the Navy by skiving, Chris lad? Ever heard of hard work never hurt anyone?'

'Yeah, I have, but thought best not to risk it. But, my, Pete, you've done well. Sorry, sir, you've done well.'

'Gets a bit of getting used to does this sir business. See you got your QR 2's. Hope you've said thank you to Bumble and John 'why did they stop the tot' Lilly.'

'Ha, ha, if they could see me now: training gunners on the old, open gun. And if they could see you—an officer and a gentleman!'

After a long natter, updating each other with our life since Gurkha, Pete thought to remind me why I hadn't reached the dizzy heights of officer status with a parting:

'Yeah, well, good to see you, Chris lad; but *I've* got work to do, even if *you* haven't.'

'Okay, Pete... sir. If I see you again I'll make sure to give you my best salute.'

'Make sure you bloody well do!'

I didn't see Pete, sir, again, but it was good to see an excellent and intelligent sailor being rewarded for his hard work.

DQ's

In early October, me and a mate of mine, George Harrison (real name Alan), who lived in a married quarter close to mine, went out one Tuesday night for a few beers.

My mother-in-law was visiting so it gave her and my wife an uninterrupted chance to natter and catch up with whatever there was to catch up with.

Well, I thought it a good excuse.

The next morning I woke up, extremely hung-over, and realised I'd slept in. After throwing on my No.8's I ran, staggered, ran to Fraser.

Reaching the top of the driveway I glanced at my watch—three minutes left. I ran, staggered, ran down the long driveway towards the barrier and guardroom. Standing behind the barrier was the quartermaster—a particularly insufferable leading seaman who I'd crossed swords with on many an occasion.

As I neared he looked at his watch. 'Will he make it? Will he make it?' he shouted as he started to walk back into the guardroom.

I went under the barrier, paused to catch my breath, then walked into the guardroom.

'You're adrift, Able Seaman...' he looked at the name strip on my shirt for conformation, '...Neylan. Two minutes adrift, to be exact. You know what time defaulters are, I take it?'

I glanced up at the guardroom clock. Dam, my watch was slow—but all the same—'Two bleedin minutes! You saw me running, for Christ's sake. What's two minutes?'

'Two minutes is two minutes—adrift. I've just logged it.'

'Well, for once in your miserable life do something decent and unlog it.'

'Carry on, sunshine, and I'll have you for insubordination.'

What with my head pounding and stomach heaving, his response tipped me over the edge.

I vented my anger by describing his unreasonable behaviour with every expletive I knew. Unfortunately, halfway through my rant, the Officer of the Watch had entered the room via the door I had my back to. With an officer present this meant that my expletive rant, by association, had also been aimed at him. And my situation could only get worse because, by being OOTW, he represented the Captain of Excellent—and by the way I was treated, probably the Lords of the Admiralty and the Queen.

'Have you finished?' the officer asked.

I turned round, realising I was in deep trouble. 'Yes, sir, sorry, sir, but I was only two...'

'Be quiet! You've said more than enough or, should I say, sworn more than enough. Quartermaster, get onto the Regulating office at Excellent and have them send transport for this, this foul mouthed rating. I'll inform his Divisional Officer and tell him why, in this case, I took the decision to forgo defaulters.'

Bloody hell: the Regulators (the Navy's infamous police). I was truly in it deep—above my head.

An hour later I found myself in Portsmouth's Detention Quarters. I'd heard stories about this barbaric place, with its punishment-led routine and swore I could smell the pain and misery imbedded in its walls.

Waiting outside the Regulators office was another poor sod. His hands were cuffed behind his back and, judging by his demeanour, I guessed this wasn't his first visit.

A Chief Petty Officer Regulator came out of the office: 'Stand to attention, you miserable pair!' he shouted, and then turned his full attention to the rating standing beside me.

Nose-to-nose, he shouted in his face, 'You don't ruddy learn, do you? For the record—rank, name, and date of birth!'

'OME Stone. March 3rd, sir.'

'What bloody year!'

'Every bloody year!'

The CR back-handed him so hard across his face I was sprayed with his snot and spittle.

'Still the cocky little sod trying to work his ticket—jumping ship will not get you out of MY Royal Navy, no matter how many times you do it. You know where to go—SO GET YOURSELF THERE—NOW!'

Bloody hell, this was worse than Ganges. The CR turned his full attention to me. 'You're Able Seaman Neylan, from Excellent...'

'Yes, chief... sir.'

'Don't interrupt me, son—NEVER INTERRUPT ME! Date of birth?'

'July 18th 1953, sir.'

'You've been remanded here 'till Monday, when you'll be before your Captain's defaulters table. You'd best pray that he doesn't send you back to me. Have you got any smoking gear?'

'Yes, sir.'

'Hand it over with anything else in your pockets, and your watch. If you're a good lad you'll get two fags a day.' He wrote my name on my half-full packet of twenty then gestured towards two leading regulators. 'Take him to his cell and fill him in on the routine.'

My cell held an iron bed, bucket, and toilet roll. There was a folded blanket on the thin, stained mattress, and one pillow that was so stained and dirty I would wrap my paper-thin pyjama top around it before I turned in.

Every evening, at 18:00—exactly 18:00, all remand detainees were crammed into the washroom. We washed ourselves and all our clothes, including our underwear, in absolute silence, then hung them in the drying room. We marched back to our cells, naked, donned our paper-thin pyjamas and turned in. The blanket was so rough it felt like sleeping with a cactus. And the cell light was left on—all night.

At 06:00 we were woken by loud shouting in the corridor, followed by the banging open of cell doors. We folded our blanket, correctly, then took our pyjamas off and folded them—correctly. We then marched naked to the drying room, retrieved our clothes, ironed them (the Ganges way), dressed, and went for breakfast. All the time being shouted at and often kicked, slapped, or punched. I later learnt that the washing clothes routine was because, being on remand, we didn't have a change of kit, unlike those doing time in the main block.

Breakfast was fun: we had a plate full of greasy food and only a spoon to eat it with—in silence. I didn't know if it was part of our punishment (but why were we being punished for an alleged offence? Some, or all of us, might well be innocent), or were knives and forks deemed as potential weapons, or to lessen the risk of self-harm?

After breakfast we strapped on a pair of gaiters and began parade drill—at the double. And it was torture—pounding round the small parade ground, sometimes with SLR's, was torture. Even on the odd occasion we came to a halt, we were never stood at ease. And if it was raining the CGI (usually a CGI) would shout at us from the cover of a vaulted doorway. I sweated so much I feared I'd end my life as a puddle.

Dinner was, just like breakfast, eaten with just a spoon; but at least we could sit down and rest our tortured muscles, and have a fag before resuming parade drill in the afternoon.

Tea consisted of a sandwich, filled with goodness knows what, accompanied by an enamelled mug of extremely weak tea, followed by our last fag of the day. Then it was off to scrub the floor of the cell before the washing routine began.

On Friday morning I was visited by my Divisional Officer and invited to give my own account of what had happened the previous Wednesday morning.

He agreed that the Quartermaster might have been over-zealous, but, he made it abundantly clear, that it didn't excuse my behaviour. He would write a report and send it to Excellent's captain. His parting words were: when asked by Excellent's Captain to explain myself, just to apologise and NOT try to offer an excuse.

Sunday was different: we only pounded the parade ground for two hours before we stopped for Church Parade. I assume, because the staff thought God might be watching, we were stood at ease to listen to somebody religious absolve us of sins we might or might not have committed.

After Church Parade we were bought to attention to listen to a CGI read the headlines of a popular newspaper, then read the football results. Obviously, by his accent, a Geordie, he tore up the newspaper when it revealed that Newcastle had been beaten by West Ham. Did Doncaster Rovers win their match? I didn't get to find out and, to be honest, didn't really care.

Early Monday morning, after being reunited with my watch and the contents of my pockets - except for the fags and loose change - I was escorted to HMS Excellent to learn my fate from her Captain. At least I'd been given access to a razor after breakfast—that was good of them.

I was marched to stand before the Captain's table (a lectern, really) by Excellent's Master-at-Arms.

'Halt! Off cap! SIR! Able Seaman Neylan.'

The Captain looked up from reading his notes and took some time staring at me. Eventually...

'Able Seaman Neylan, I've read the charges and the report from your DO. Do you understand the charges?'

Charges? Bloody hell, they've included the two minutes adrift. Two bloody minutes!

Self preservation. 'Yes, SIR.'

'You're married and live in North End, I take it?'

'Actually, sir, I now have a married quarter in ...'

'I don't care where the bloody hell you live! You're behaviour was deplorable. Unacceptable, thoroughly unacceptable. What have you to say for yourself?'

I remembered my DO's parting words. 'My behaviour *was* unacceptable, SIR, and I apologise, SIR.'

'Humph, you have a relatively good behaviour record and your DO is satisfied with your work at Fraser. However, your behaviour WAS unacceptable. Ten days number nines. Think yourself lucky and don't, don't ever appear before my table again. Dismissed!'

'On cap - about turn - quick march!'

Ten days nines seemed a reasonable result—I was truly thankful with not being given a trip back to DQ's. But, all the same, I did feel aggrieved—two minutes—two bloody minutes.

Nines meant punishment and stoppage of leave, so I was given a bed and locker in the punishment mess at Excellent. Once back at Fraser I'd been allowed to go home and collect the kit I'd need for nine days. Half an hour I had. Just one second over and I would be AWOL, which would mean a return for a much longer stay at DQ's. I wasn't late back—I was early.

Those under punishment would muster on Galley square at the end of every training day. After a bout of parade drill - at the double - we would be set to work. This could be sweeping roads and walkways, emptying rubbish bins, or cleaning in the galley and dining room - finishing at 19:00.

Weekends were much the same except the drill and work would last all day; but at least we were finished by 17:00. But being under punishment meant we couldn't avail ourselves of any of Excellent's leisure venues—we were limited to a small, vending machine facility.

Added to my misery was that, every week-day morning, the RN bus transporting staff and trainees from Excellent to Fraser would pass a bus stop where I would see my wife waiting to catch her bus to work in North End.

Two bloody minutes!

At the age of twenty-one, due to an ever-shrinking fleet, I was given the option of leaving the Royal Navy if I transferred to the Royal Navy Fleet Reserve (special class) to finish my twelve years service. It was almost a year after my DQ's experience, and I was still smarting over those 'two bloody

201

minutes'. Plus, I was due another draft chit; a draft that would almost certainly be to a sea-going ship.

My wife, understandably, was reluctant to be left alone in Portsmouth, far from her family.

So, with some regret, I left the Navy and ventured forth to Civvie Street. I did, however, have to lug my entire kit home to Doncaster and keep it fully serviceable for the next five years in case of future conflict. Where upon I would be called to come to the rescue of my Queen and country.

Finally...

I am now a relatively old man, adrift, like my peers, in the present where progress has spelt the end of Royal Navy establishments like HMS Ganges and, in my opinion, discipline has been the cost of progress.

I have watched numerous documentaries about life onboard modern Royal Navy ships and in training establishments, and was somewhat dismayed to see how much general discipline and self-discipline has declined.

However, it is true that each generation judges the next generation by their own standards—the 'Old Salts' of yesteryear would probably have found the Royal Navy I served in wanting.

Nevertheless, after watching the commissioning of HMS Queen Elizabeth on television, I was disappointed to see that some Junior Ratings hadn't positioned their cap tallies correctly. Who inspected them before the ceremony? It certainly wasn't a good, old-fashioned, Chief Gunnery Instructor.

After leaving the Royal Navy I had a few factory jobs before following my brothers and father down a coal mine.

When most of the mines were closed in the early 1990's, I went to college, hoping to acquire some A levels and become a social worker - a social worker because I'd spent a few years volunteering for the Samaritans. However, I'd acquired enough A levels to train as a teacher at Sheffield Hallam University.

After four years of academically demanding work, I qualified as a Bachelor of Education, specialising in early years English, Drama, and Dance.

I retired in 2014 after, I hope, making learning fun for many children.

Acknowledgements

First to thank is my daughter, Jennifer, who suggested I write my Royal Navy memoirs in book form, rather than give her a folder of documents and pictures to keep for my grandson, who'd have to rely on his imagination and tales I'd told his mother if I was no longer around to bring the documents and pictures to life.

I am most grateful to Les Fisher (former Able Seaman, RP2, and Navigators Yeoman) whose memory of his time at Ganges and, indeed, his memory of all the time he spent in the Navy, far exceed my own. He was also very helpful with the chapter on HMS Torquay, having served in HMS - wandering - Whitby. He also provided the title!

Much appreciated is the help I received from John Lilly. A much valued messmate and mentor onboard HMS Gurkha. If ever there was a rating that epitomised the steadfast and disciplined attitude of the Royal Navy in the 1970's, John is that rating.

I am also indebted to David Axford (www.axfordsabode) for his guidance in acquiring some of the Ganges photographs; and to Reg Bailey for giving his permission to use some of the same. And a huge thank you to all former Ganges ratings who have posted their experiences on the World Wide Web.

And, of course, thanks and gratitude to all of the remarkable Royal Navy personnel I trained and served with.

Finally, for their interest, encouragement, and patience—love and gratitude to Jane, Clair, Sue Raspin, Big Al, and Floyd Dunkerley.

Printed in Great Britain
by Amazon